Thank you for buying the second edition of the Football and Real Ale Guide,

I have improved this guide thanks to the comments of the readers of last year's guides.

Pub selection criteria

The pubs are selected if they have been recommended to me as:-

- Friendly to visiting away fans
- Have a good selection of well kept real ale.
- Are located close, but not too close to the ground
- In each town I tried to get a balance of large, small, good food and community based pubs
- I have visited every pub and talked to those in charge

The maps

The new maps locate the pubs and the grounds. They were compiled under licence by Dotted Eyes of Bromsgrove.

The pub descriptions

The beer list is now organised in alphabetical order of the brewer and then beer. Ciders are given if they are on draught, after the beers.

The new food descriptions are direct quotations from the landlord. I do not sample food but take the advice of the locals as to the best pub to combine the beer with a meal.

I also now give pub opening times. They give closing times but, as with all pubs, they have freedom to extend the hours beyond those given here.

Taxis

I have included a list of taxis numbers in the guide. They are not recommendations but are often ones that I used over the year.

The Photographs

All photographs were taken by myself and on the day of my visit except where I visited late in the evening and had to return the next morning.

Awards

Throughout the guide you will find pages that indicate that some pubs are deserving of extra recognition. The divisional awards were voted for by readers and those I met in my choices. No pub receives any financial benefit from being entered or given an award. Likewise no pub has paid any money to be included. The awards are just a bit of fun.

League tables

The league tables of last year certainly created some comment over the year and especially so in the towns that were near the bottom of the league. They are included again by popular demand and are slightly more sophisticated because I have tried to balance the number of ales in the pubs with the number of alternatives in the town.

Cultural Guides

I am really pleased that Glyn accepted my offer to write for the guides. When you read the pages please do so in the spirit in which they were written. How often have you thought about going to an away game only to think that there will be time to fill before opening, people and friends to consider or, what else can I find to justify the trip? How often late in the evening have you found yourself looking for something to say about a place that you have visited and wanted something more to say than 'The beer was good'? Glyn might just give you some excuses/topics of conversation/trivia that could get you a pass out the next time you wish to visit.

Some comments may offend. In this case they are all Glyn's and writs should be sent to him. At other times you will be amused and then congratulatory notes can be sent to me. At all times the guides offer an alternative look at British cities by someone who describes himself as 'permanently angry with things that don't really matter.' Unfortunately, however, some of the comments do matter and without people getting angry in a typically British way then much of what we love in the urban landscape will be lost. Should you ever meet Glyn I do offer some advice. Don't get into a conversation about Pylons. Life is just too short.

The Website

The website offers the best place to order, buy and comment on the pubs.
www.footballandrealaleguide.co.uk

Stedders June 2006

I never visit a place before reviewing it, it prejudices a man so.
Adapted from a quote by Sydney Smith (1771-1845)

I wrote the first Bradwan Cultural Guide for the City Gent in 2001 and about half the Guides here are rewrites of Gent articles, so there are variations in style. I did not write them to please an imaginary audience, but to share my enthusiasms and occasionally my anger. From an early age I visited places because I was curious about everything. When I started drinking beer and travelling to away games I continued to explore the towns I was drinking and watching in. I have no problem fitting real ale, football and culture together in my head, and hope what I have written will be of some interest to most, and raise a smile and some enthusiasm in at least a few.

I believe there are good and dreadful ways to run most things including football clubs and towns. Websites that freeze my computer or have no links for visitors are annoying: and getting lost when sober because there are no maps, signposts or street names suggests a badly managed place; especially where millions have been spent on nagging notices. People warm to friendly welcomes, but are less likely to return if they are abused, or treated like savages or idiots.

The Guides are around 250 words, which limited the web links and information I could include. Please check everything for yourself. If you end up outside a locked and rain soaked attraction with a complaining significant other and grizzling parental responsibilities it's your fault.

One author found particularly useful was Simon Inglis. His *The Football Grounds of Great Britain* was the first and best of its kind, and his latest, *Engineering Archie*, provided much historical background, especially for London. Glyn Watkins' dubious biography

Like Richard Stedman I support a struggling football club, drink proper beer, did time in teaching, and am a publisher. Unlike him I sometimes cook, can go days without visiting the pub, draw, write poetry and occasionally get angry. I created my first book *Walburgas forgetting – forgiving* when pneumonia stopped me supply teaching, and left me too ill for anything physical but not ill enough to sleep all day. To stop me going mad, or madder, I made a book of some drawings and poems I had done over 20 years. When I got better I made and sold about a hundred more. After being awarded a business start up grant I published them, and organised a launch at the *National Museum of Photography, Film & Television*. This involved me finding the last remaining print of a film called *A Month in the Country*, based on a book by JL Carr and starring Colin Firth, Natasha Richardson and Kenneth Branagh. I also persuaded Channel 4 to release it on DVD for the first time.

I produced my second book, *The Wayne Jacobs Little Red Head Book – A Red Headed Footballer & the Mysteries of Red Hair* because Wayne Jacobs is a decent bloke and footballer whose testimonial year was seemingly being forgotten because Bradford City being in administration, again. I sold hundreds and gave over £200 to Wayne's testimonial fund. I have also done other handmade books, including *Highway to ULL. Hayseed Dixie, hillbilly rock, highlands, alcohol, Finland & fish*, when I was Poet in Residence at the first Loopallu festival in Ullapool.

I have done a few other things, including creating a JB Priestley Night, which involved piping in a meat and potato pie with a cornet playing On Ilkley Moor Baht'at. I am presently working on a documentary script and connected book entitled: Lines of Power – Lines of Pleasure. The history and poetry of pylons.

Visit *www.bradwan.com* for more about me and to buy my books

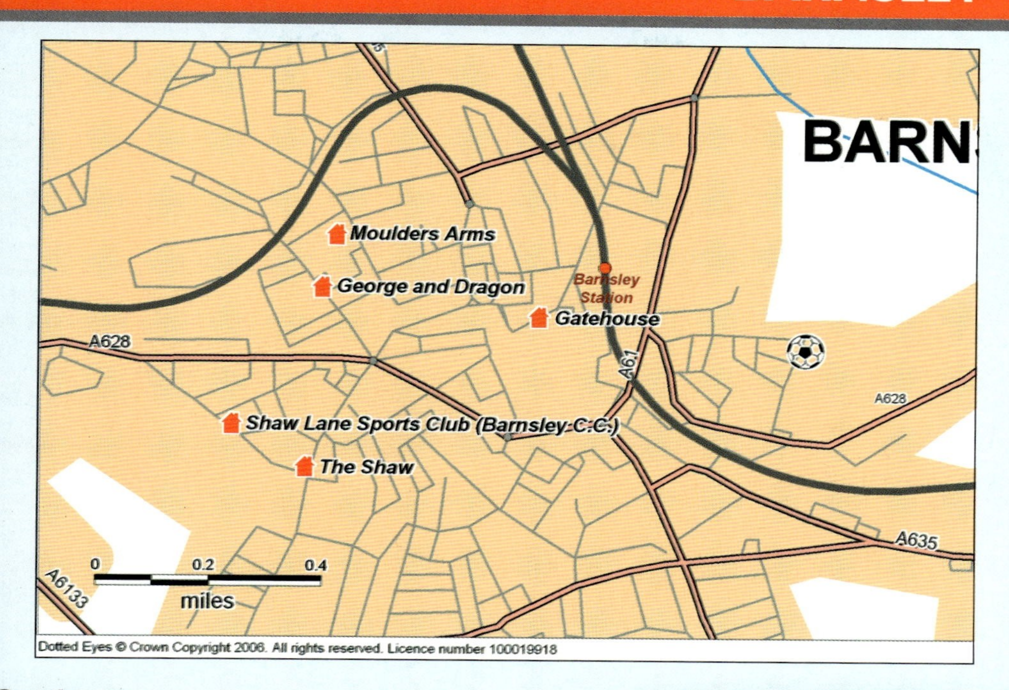

Gatehouse

35 Eldon Street S70 2JJ. Telephone 01226 282394 New
Gaffer: Robert Rudge
Food: Good homely food with true value in both special and main menu
12 to 2.30, 5 to 7 Mon to Fri, 12 to 3.30 Sat
Separate smoking areas
Open: 11 to 11 Mon to Thu, 11 to 12 Fri to Sat, Closed Sun

B F

MP TV BM

The Good Real Ale Doctor ordered that Barnsley town centre needed major surgery. Pubs were dying and the fizzy medicine was having no positive effect. Then Robert came to the rescue and the Gatehouse has opened to revive the flagging beast that is a good Barnsley pub scene. The pub has a great location, opposite the inevitable Interchange just five minutes walk from the ground and conveniently out of the main town lager streets.

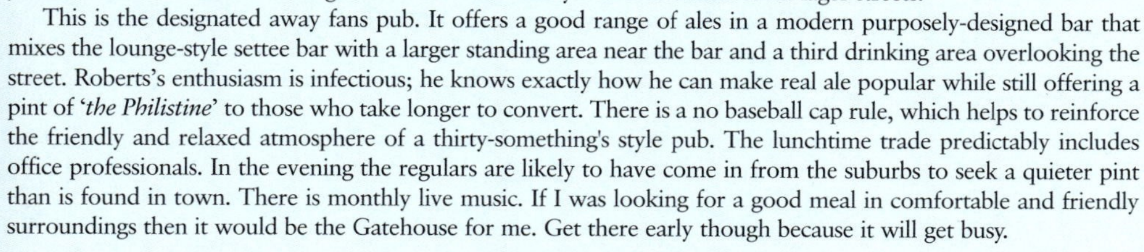

This is the designated away fans pub. It offers a good range of ales in a modern purposely-designed bar that mixes the lounge-style settee bar with a larger standing area near the bar and a third drinking area overlooking the street. Roberts's enthusiasm is infectious; he knows exactly how he can make real ale popular while still offering a pint of '*the Philistine*' to those who take longer to convert. There is a no baseball cap rule, which helps to reinforce the friendly and relaxed atmosphere of a thirty-something's style pub. The lunchtime trade predictably includes office professionals. In the evening the regulars are likely to have come in from the suburbs to seek a quieter pint than is found in town. There is monthly live music. If I was looking for a good meal in comfortable and friendly surroundings then it would be the Gatehouse for me. Get there early though because it will get busy.

BWV 10.5.06: Acorn ***Darkness***, Greene King ***Old Speckled Hen***, John Smith's ***Cask Bitter***, Springhead ***Roaring Meg***, Wentworth ***Bumble Bee***

George and Dragon

41-43 Summer Lane, S70 2NW. Telephone 01226 205609
Gaffer: Keith McManis
Smoking Throughout
Open: 12 to 11, 12 to 10.30 Sun

In the short time that Keith has been at the George and Dragon he has met a local demand for the golden ales among the Barnsley faithful. In doing so the pub is a welcome standard bearer for local ales that others might try to emulate. Two rooms are found on different levels, the upper room being a pool room and bar. I settled in the lower bar with others getting into a horse racing afternoon. The décor is very country-farmhouse style with carpet and upholstered seats and the now slimmed-down tea pot collection as mentioned in the CAMRA guide entry. I returned a day later, the pub was so welcoming; the beer was equally good as the first pint of the day was pulled. This is a very friendly and popular pub, getting busiest in the post-work rush hour. While I was there the order of the day was indeed plenty of the Golden Pippin. So it made a great complementary location to the Moulders Arms, literally a hundred yards up the road. This is the place for a lunchtime pool and ale session.
UPDATE: The beer selection is narrower but the quality still good.

BWV 15.3.05: Acorn ***Barnsley Gold***, Copper Dragon ***Golden Pippin***, John Smith's ***Cask Bitter***
BWV 10.5.06: John Smith's ***Cask Bitter***, Flowers ***IPA***

Moulders Arms

49 Summer Street, S70 2NU. Telephone 01226 215767
Gaffer: Kevin Davis
Smoking Throughout
Open: 4.30 to 11 Mon to Thu, 2.30 to 11 Fri, 12 to 11 Sat, 12 to 10.30 Sun

This is a classic locals' pub that would be welcome in all streets in Barnsley, if only! This is a rarity in smooth keg land and as a result it is a very popular local. I arrived just after the 4.30 weekday opening and enjoyed a very pleasant chat and personal gamble on the Cheltenham Festival racing on the TV Kevin offers a guest beer to the regulars that change within the week and the quality is such that it deserves the pub of the season award. The low rooms are host to regular darts, quizzes and, curiously, a buskers' night. Do as the slogan says and stagger inn to Kevin and Irene's pub. It will be really welcoming, a great oasis in the Barnsley ale desert. Curiously this is the only entry in the CAMRA guide for Barnsley. There is a mini pub crawl to be had on Summer Lane and the distance into town isn't so great, especially as the ground is literally up the hill from the railway station. So why not settle in here for a few, and avoid the bustle of a traditional Yorkshire town centre Saturday.
UPDATE: A marquee is now up in the pub garden. The pub has remained the same evn though it is now moved to Enterprise ownership.

BWV 15.3.05: Greene King ***IPA***, John Smith's ***Cask Bitter***, York ***Yorkshire Terrier***
BWV 10.5.06: Greene King ***Ruddles Best***, John Smith's ***Cask Bitter***

The Shaw

Racecommon Road S70 6AE. Telephone 01226 294021
Gaffer: Tara Gilroy
Smoking Throughout
Open: 3.30 to 12 Mon to Fri, 12 to 12 Sat, 12 to 11 Sun

New to the pub game and making an impressive impression on the real ale scene is this grand pub on the way into town. Because they liked the place so much, Angela and James have moved from being punters to landlords. It is easy to see why as the scale of the place is inspiring. The best room is nearest the door where a great fire was surrounded by locals sampling ale and spending plenty on the quality juke box selection. There are four large rooms, all with high ceilings and tastefully, yet simply decorated. The back room has a second pool table but is not recommended unless you are very very young, i.e. under five. The Shaw is a place to sit, read a paper, etc. but I suspect a party will often break out without much prompting. On leaving it was appropriate that as my last pint in Barnsley was sunk, a repeat of the Pogues '*Dirty Old Town*' was thumping out. The community was mourning one of their finest in appropriate pub style, one of the traditions that make great community pubs.
UPDATE: The pub has been redecorated and '*turns*' are a regular feature on Fridays, as are quiz, darts and pool nights.

BWV 15.3.05: Greene King ***IPA***, John Smith's ***Cask Bitter***, Marston's ***Pedigree***
BWV 10.5.06: Acorn ***Barnsley Bitter***, ***Old Moor Porter***

Shaw Lane Sports Club (Barnsley C.C.)

New

Shaw Lane, S70 6HZ Telephone 01226 203509
Gaffer: Roy Robinson
Food: Bar snacks and Sunday lunches 6 to 9.30, 12 to 3 Sun
Smoking Throughout
Opening Times: 4.45 to 11 Mon to Fri, 11.30 to 11 Sat and Sun

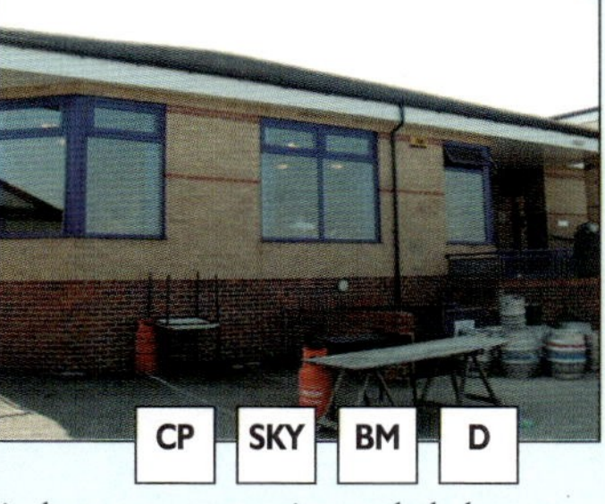

The Shaw Lane Sports Club bar has been given the Cricket Club sub - title because the bar overlooks one of the most famous Yorkshire league squares and will draw appreciation from any cricket lovers who know the roots of Mssrs, Gough, Bird and Boycott. It is a proper social club catering for sportsmen and women in many events from archery to athletics. Unlike the typical sports club it is, however, a genuine real ale bar housed in a sparkling bright new pavilion.

There are two rooms. The front bar overlooks the cricket and is light and airy, laid out ready for cricket tea type activity. The larger back bar is the home for regular functions such as weddings and parties. Both offer good value for the member who pays their £5 a year membership. I distracted Roy, the bar manager, from his squash coaching and soon we were chatting about his obvious love of what the bar has recently achieved. It has won CAMRA club awards and seems open to the local community who might like to trek up the drive whenever it is open. The club house has been here for six years and its ale pedigree includes a confidence that encourages the regulars to suggest guest ales. There will always be a Wentworth ale and other surprises found on the members' travels. I decided to get the full cricket experience and sit in the seated enclosure while writing these notes. The groundsman toiled away creating that perfect finish; someone should give him free beer for life.

BWV 10.5.06: Acorn ***Darkness***, Phoenix ***Wobbly Bob***, Wentworth ***Best***

Barnsley

Things have changed here since the dark days of the young Michael Parkinson. Barnsley has slightly trendy bars next to the 1930's town hall, and a new bus station.

Monk Bretton Priory

These free to enter low set ruins stand in the verdant grasslands of a council estate, a short walk from Oakwell along Thorpe Park Linear Park. Everything worth more than a wooden groat was carted away for Henry VIII in the original English de-nationalisation. The priory belonged to the Clunic order and was an observant, or "rock hard" monastery. At the dissolution the monks carried on praying together in a private house. There was nothing to stop other monks doing the same, but apart from a few rebels that lost their head and lost their heads, most took jobs as priests or retired on the pensions they were bribed with. If you know nothing about monastic architecture and have a relative working in TV you could become a television expert and read an autocue. Alternatively, if you have children you can buy them a book about monasteries and pretend interest when they explain it all to you.

You will pass a mobile home franchise on your way to Oakwell. It is a poor area in a poor town, and this place does not sell cheap VW campers that Aussies can afford; but trucks like the Simpson's Ultimate Behemoth. A mobile home here will probably cost more than a normal, stays roughly were it was built, house down the street.

Birmingham

Birmingham claims to have more canals than Venice, which is true, but Venice's canals are squeezed into the jewel of the Adriatic, whereas Birmingham's are spread across the grey, breeze blocked centre of Britain. Birmingham started as a small market town on the border of three counties, allowing dodgy market traders to nip across a county boundary if the law came along.

Good Things

The Art Gallery and Museum is one of the finest in the country. The Pinto wood collection alone is worth a trip. Commercially, Birmingham is obviously booming. There were fewer charity shops then even Kensington has.
www.birmingham.org.uk

Bad Things

This is a soul destroying monument to mammon which sacrificed people to cars and corruption. New Street station, and the numerous pedestrian underpasses, makes strangers feel like they are walking around an Esher engraving of a 19th century sewer. If you tried to grow mushrooms in New Street the Cruelty Free Fungus Campaign would object. The train information was inadequate, the platforms too narrow, the escalators did not work, and the stairs were not safe. Once you escaped to the street Birmingham apparently believed directions are just for decoration. You could search for something until the concrete crumbled for all Birmingham cared. Brummies are probably not much better off. The few public maps were surrounded by crowds trying to work out where they on Earth they were. We have not experienced Birmingham for three years so it may have improved, and soon beer may be free.

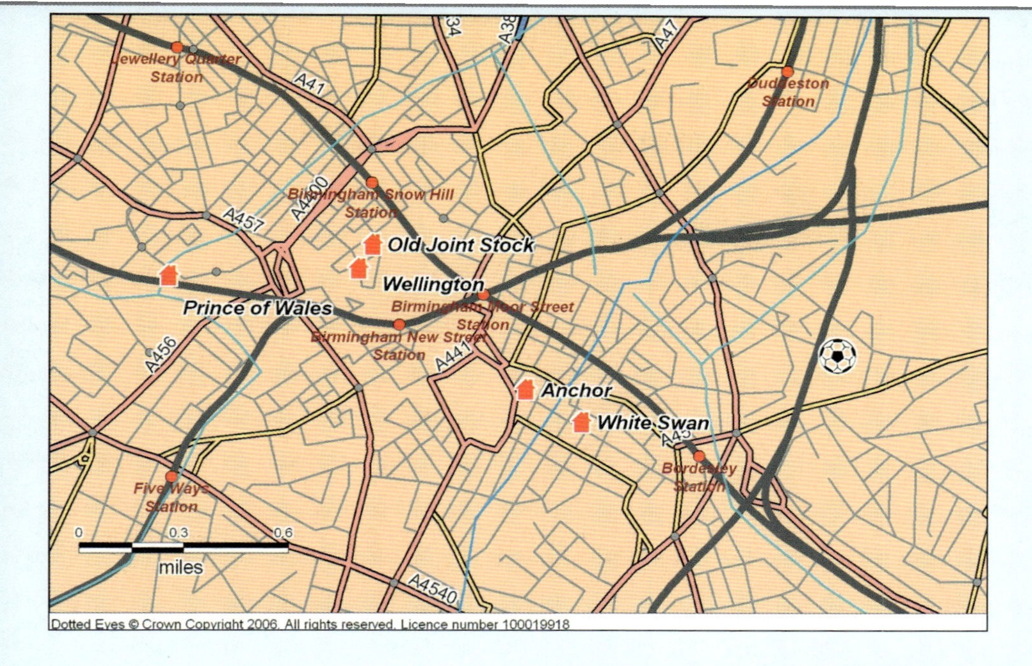

Anchor

308 Bradford Street, Digbeth, B5 6ET. Telephone 0121 622 4516
www.theanchorinnbirmingham.co.uk
Gaffer: Gerry Keane
Food: Typical pub menu from 12 to 8
Two separate no-smoking bars
Open: 11 to late

MP | TV | JB | PG | D

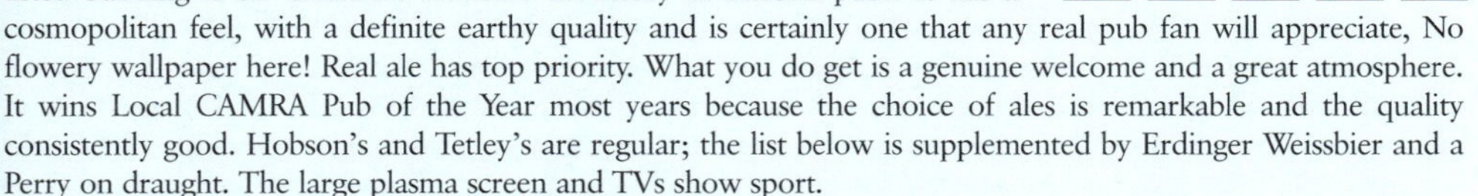

Pub of the year awards are celebrated here, as the tradition for top-quality ale continues to draw those venturing just beyond the new Bull Ring. This grade II listed building is on CAMRA's National Inventory of historic pubs. It has a cosmopolitan feel, with a definite earthy quality and is certainly one that any real pub fan will appreciate, No flowery wallpaper here! Real ale has top priority. What you do get is a genuine welcome and a great atmosphere. It wins Local CAMRA Pub of the Year most years because the choice of ales is remarkable and the quality consistently good. Hobson's and Tetley's are regular; the list below is supplemented by Erdinger Weissbier and a Perry on draught. The large plasma screen and TVs show sport.
UPDATE: Gerry has returned to the helm full time and the traditions of the Anchor remain in place.

BWV 20.2.05: Beartown ***Pandamonium***, Brown Cow ***Old E'fer***, Cannon Royall ***Arrowhead***, Foxield ***White Fox***, Greene King ***Abbot***, Hambleton ***Nightmare***, Hanby ***Coopers Mild***, Rooster's ***Brewers Gold***, Skinner's ***Tinners***, Wye Valley ***White Knuckle***, Cheddar Valley ***Traditional Cider***
BWV 9.11.05: Florette ***Blonde***, Hampshire ***Victory's Home***, Hepworth ***Organic Cool Blonde Lager***, Hobsons ***Old Henry***, ***Mild***, Kelham Island ***Workhouse Henry***, Pictish ***Z-Rod***, Rooster's ***Bullet***, Salamander ***Dreadnought***, Thatcher's ***Cheddar Valley Cider***

F

MP TV BM

Old Joint Stock

4 Temple Row West B2 5NY. Telephone 0121 200 1892
www.fullers.co.uk

New

Gaffer: Alison Turner
Food: Ale and Pie pub (Traditional English) from 12 onwards
Smoking Throughout
Open: 11 to 11 Mon to Sat, Closed Sunday

The Old Joint Stock will strike a happy chord with those Londoners who hanker after a bit of home in the Midlands. It is a Fuller's pub in the grand style. Converted 8 years ago, it retains the scale and majesty found in similar pubs in their chain, such as Fleet Street's Old Bank of England. Panelled library rooms lead off a massive central bar and the view through the large picture windows is of the cathedral and locals busying their way to pray or, more likely, to work. Unofficially, this is the staff-room for the Wellington (*see Aston Villa entry*) next door and it was with some joy I shared a pint with Nigel who introduced me to Geoff, the Plymouth fan and pub manager.

Be aware of two facts. The pub is not open on Sundays, and the signs relating to no scarves, baseball caps, or football shirts are enforced. My lunchtime visit was typical as the place was well represented by suits and couples '*doing lunch*'. A gentle murmur pervaded the large rooms. There is ample space for your conversation to be lost in the ether. Saturdays bring shoppers, many women and well-heeled footie fans. It will be interesting to see how the themed ale festivals are received. The touch of London life is now established in the psyche of the second city. Good ale, glorious surroundings and a distinct lack of geezers to turn the beer sour.

BWV 9.11.05: Beowulf ***Beorma***, Fuller's ***Chiswick***, ***Discovery***, ***ESB***, ***IPA***, ***Trafalgar***

MP TV BM D

Prince of Wales

84 Cambridge Street, Five Ways, B1 2ND. Telephone 0121 643 9460
Gaffer: Mark Pagett
Food: Quality English Food 12 to 7

New

Smoking Throughout
Open: 11 to 11, 11 to 10.30 Sun

On Nigel's recommendation I made the handy trek out to the Convention Centre to find what he described as a bit of good old Birmingham that still remains among the new developments. It is a real find. Just off Broad Street, it could be in a totally different world to the brash bars of the new canal-side eateries that also do beer.

The first thing that struck me on entry to the single bar was the faint smell of my Granddad's pipe tobacco rather than cigarette smoke. The Woodbines signs on the wall were a further endorsement of the old-fashioned values that continue in this friendly local. The beer quality was excellent and obviously popular with the local regulars, visiting concert performers and walkers, yes walkers, who could well have tied up nearby. The pub has a deliberately distressed look often found in your classic village local. Strangers quickly become like long-lost friends and nothing is too much trouble. Even the choice of live music is a bit quirky. In this case next up was the Clarksville Mountain Band, typical of the blues/folk enjoyed on a Sunday night. The Prince of Wales is sister pub to the nearby Stage, yet draws more than its fair share of concert-goers and performers. No doubt the new licensing laws will be very useful for a pub such as this.

BWV 9.11.05: Adnams ***Broadside***, Ansells ***Bitter***, ***Mild***, Brains ***SA***, Greene King ***Abbot***, Springhead ***Charlie's Angel***, Timothy Taylor ***Landlord***, Wells ***Bombardier***

The Wellington

37 Bennets Hill, B2 5SN. Telephone 0121 2003115
G Nigel Barker

Separate smoking areas
Open: 10 to 12, 11 to 12 Sun

Fancy a fiver on the Wellington being CAMRA pub of the year in the next few years? This is the sort of acclaim that has come to the Wellington, and it is not yet a year old. The pub was a must-visit as soon as recommendations for new pubs came my way. 2,200 beers in a year, all different! The beers change as you move along the bar. The turnover is such that drinking by numbers is literally the order of the day.

The Wellington is a single bar in a great location that stretches deep to the back where a non-smoking section is found. An impressive frontage belies its former night-club past, but it is the landlord's dream of quality ale in a city-centre street that we should all appreciate.. No music, no fruit machines, etc. Have you heard that before? In the Wellington you wouldn't want them. It is though, a real pub. Frequented by fans of all clubs in the Midlands, the talk is typically self-deprecating. Arsenal fans paid it high regard on their latest visit. Let's hope the dour predictions do not mean it is lost to the premiership next year. Surely not!

BWV 9.11.05: Black Country ***BFG***, Fireside, ***Pig on the Wall***, Cairngorm ***Blessed Thistle***, Craftsman ***Eel Catcher***, Downton ***Light Fantastic***, Fullmash ***Vamp***, Hampshire ***Pendragon***, Kelham Island ***Brown Ale***, Milk Street ***Autumn Moon***, Pictish ***Samhain Stout***, St. Austell ***Tinners Ale***, Saddlers ***Stumbling Badger***, Salopian ***Hop Devil***, Scattor Rock ***Proper Job***, ***Working Mary's Brown Ale*** Saxon ***Purple Haze Cider***, Sheppy ***Kingston Black Cider***, Barkers ***Upsy Daisy Perry***

White Swan

276 Bradford Street, Digbeth B12 0QY. Telephone 0121 622 2586
Gaffer: Agnes Cretton
Food: Sandwiches and pies
Smoking Throughout
Open: 11 to 3, 4 to 11, 11 to 11 Fri to Sun

This is cracking pub. It is a place where the architecture adds interest but doesn't distract from the serious beer revelry. Spot the similarities with the photo of the Bartons Arms. While we watched a game on Sky the locals were readily willing to chat about beer, sport in general and just how good this pub is. There is a genuine Irish angle to the entertainment on offer. It is also heaving on matchdays so get there early, but not in colours, because, whilst the locals will make you more than welcome, others on Bradford Street may be less generous in their greetings. I loved this pub and would visit whenever in town. The landlord certainly looks after these locals – they were last heard planning their annual trip to watch an Irish rugby international, this time in Paris. Several beers later I forced myself, with some reluctance, to leave the comfort of my corner seat in the White Swan, to check out the less attractive city centre trendy ale houses.
UPDATE: Agnes continues to run a top local; another good hour was spent with friendly Brummies. Nothing has changed, and hopefully never will.

BWV 20.2.05: Banks's ***Bitter***, ***Original***, ***Mild***
BWV 9.11.05: Banks's ***Bitter***, ***Original***

Plans are in place for you to be involved in writing for the Guides.

We already have a team of football fans who would like to share their experiences of drinking real ale when following their team.

I am offering a small payment to cover the cost of beer and transport when you research the pubs

You will not get rich doing this, neither will I

We would like you to join the team

It could be that you compile the entries for your own town

Maybe you might write about your favourites

You may even wish to rewrite my entries as they should be written
You can write as many or as little as we agree.

GO ON
JOIN THE TEAM

WRITE THE ALL NEW FOOTBALL AND REAL ALE GUIDES

JUST CONTACT ME
via email at r.stedman1@btinternet.com
OR by telephone at 01844 343931

THERE WILL NOT BE ANOTHER GUIDE UNLESS YOU HELP TO WRITE IT

THE 2007-08 GUIDES WILL BE EVEN BETTER FOR IT

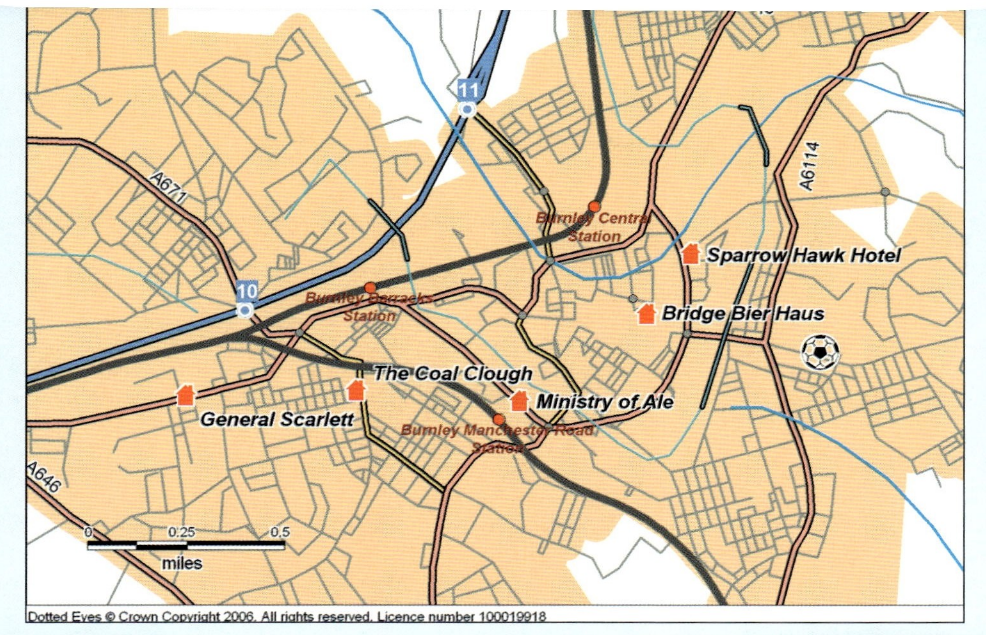

Bridge Bier Huis

2 Bank Parade, BB11 1UH. Telephone 01282 411304
www.thebridgebierhaus.co.uk
Gaffer: Simon Scott
Smoking Throughout
Closed Mon to Tue, Open 12 to 11 Wed to Fri,. 11 to 11 Sat, 12 ro 10.30 Sun
Open from 5 on Tue if Burnley are at home

The Bier Huis is just outside the town centre and convenient for the central station and walk a to the ground. This back - street corner bar has an updated traditional look with café furniture, yet retaining a bar with snug layout. It is often packed, with Clarets from distant supporters clubs, who meet up here. Also try the masses of continental beers. During the day the pub is a serious ale house, no music or games to divert the supper from ale and good conversation. But it is also well known for acoustic nights when this pub will be packed. Similarly at 2 before a game the faithful have yet to depart' leaving it in notorious Turf Moor style at 10 to 3 "and returning again at 5" (again at 4.30 in some seasons.) The trendiness of the Bridge extends to real ale fashion by offering 40 plus European bottled ales and speciality lagers alongside the ever - changing microbrews.
UPDATE: The pub has proven to be the division's most popular pub among the readers who voted in my 06 - 07 online poll. Closed when I visited as it was a Tuesday Doh! European draft ales include Leffe Blonds, St Louis Kriek, Erdinger and Budvar.

BWV 17.12.04: 3 Rivers ***IPA***, Archers ***Seasonal Greetings***, Bowland ***Baa Humbug***, Hydes Bitter, Saxon ***Midnight Hour Cider***
BWV: 12.06.06: Cottage ***Germany Calling***, Everards ***Svengal Tiger***, Hydes ***Original***, Milestone ***Black Pearl***, Three B's ***Bee on the Ball***

The Coal Clough

41 Coal Clough Lane, BB11 4PG. Telephone 01282 423226
Gaffers: Bob and Pat Duckworth
Smoking Throughout
Open: 12 to 12

The Coal Clough, along with the General Scarlett were pubs that I would like to have entered in last year's guides but I concentrated on the town centre for that edition. The Coal Clough comes highly recommended by Burnley folk as a great community local and an essential visit for those undertaking a best of Burnley pub crawl.

The pub is high on the hill that lies between the motorway and town centre. The local area is one of terraced streets and has a typical friendly feel. Bob and Pat have been here for years, and since 2000 as landlord and lady. The beer list has three regulars that include the Massey's ale. This is unusual in itself. Bob and the locals will tell you the details of how and why this is the only outlet for the name. The pub will be undergoing a redecoration over the next year. At present it is very blue. There are two traditionally styled rooms, a great back room that is a games room without a pool table, i.e. the locals love to play card games, darts and dominoes. The main bar is longer and similarly comfortable in the carpeted lounge style. The pub is busy in the evenings especially when the quiz nights are held or when live music takes up the end of the room that has stage lighting. The football fans that use this pub include Bob, who was happy to share his experiences of watching the Dons with me. The Coal Clough will be a very friendly mid point for that aforementioned pub crawl.

BWV 6.06.06: Cains ***Bitter***, Shepherd Neame ***Kent's Best***, Tower ***Massey's Original Ale***, ***Whistleblower***, Worthington ***Best***

General Scarlett

243 Accrington Road, BB11 5ET Telephone 01282 831054
Gaffer: Lynne Murton
Smoking Throughout
Open: 12 to 2 Tue to Thu, 11 to 12 Fri and Sat

No trip to Burnley would be complete without a visit to the tap room of the Moorhouse's brewery. The photo was taken from the brewery car park and indeed my first visit found the pub totally refurbished and the full list of ales on offer. Lynne has been here for nine years or so and has been host not only to the locals but also to the many who visit the brewery and the bar that doubles as a shop window. The refurbishment is very well done, especially in the way that real ale enthusiasts can share in the successes of the brewery. The awards, including that for one of their national champion beers, are displayed in the modern yet cosy snug near the pub door. Mum was proud to point out a photo of her son hauling barrels for the brewery as a new employee seventeen years ago. The sense of community involvement continues within the fantastic games room at the back of the pub. This is also a trophy room for the many pub teams and apparently the older boys who use the pub can recognise their relatives in photos of long-gone Clarion Club cricket teams.

The beer is the major pull here. This is the highest and most distant point of the crawl. I would start here, especially if I had arrived from the motorway because it is all down hill to town. There will be a few football fans in on a lunchtime, many of whom will be similarly interested in swapping tales of real ale. They are used to welcoming strangers to their local and so it would be rude not to join them.

BWV 6.06.06: Moorhouses ***Black Cat***, ***Blond Witch***, ***Pendle Witches Brew***, ***Pride of Pendle***, ***Premier***

Ministry of Ale

9 Trafalgar Street, BB11 1TQ. Telephone 01282 830909
www.ministryofales.co.uk
Gaffer: Mick Jacques
Smoking Throughout
Open: 5 to 11 Mon to Thu, Closed Wed, 12 to 11 Fri and Sat, 12 to 10.30 Sun

SP

I had one of the top hours of the year in the company of Mick and some not-so-local regulars. He told me it has been a pub since 1860 and was rebuilt when the brewery made this their taphouse. This pub, with brewery attached, has it all for people like me who revel in the stories of brewery renaissance. While tiny, it draws in regulars from far and near and offers guests to complement their own varieties. Everything in the pub convinces you that the beer is strong but it isn't. Nothing is square, the floor is uneven. The tables are lovingly made by the landlord who holds centre stage in the personally designed apex of the bar. It all adds to the charm of the place. I wish their beers could be found in other pubs. But demand here is so great it rarely happens. The pub also *'holds great art exhibitions;'* on my visit it included photos of pubs old and new. So to the back bar I ventured, ale in hand, to spend time admiring pictures of Burnley's lost boozers.
UPDATE: The pub is still brilliant. It too was closed when I visited, i.e. it doesn't open until 5. Moonstone beers and guests are the norm.

BWV 17.12.04: King Alfred's ***Hampshire Bitter***, Moonstone ***Craggy's***, ***Wobble***, Young's ***Special***
BWV.2.6.06: Derwent ***Summer Rose***, Harviestoun ***Schiehallion***, Moonstone ***Black Star***, ***Pale Amber***

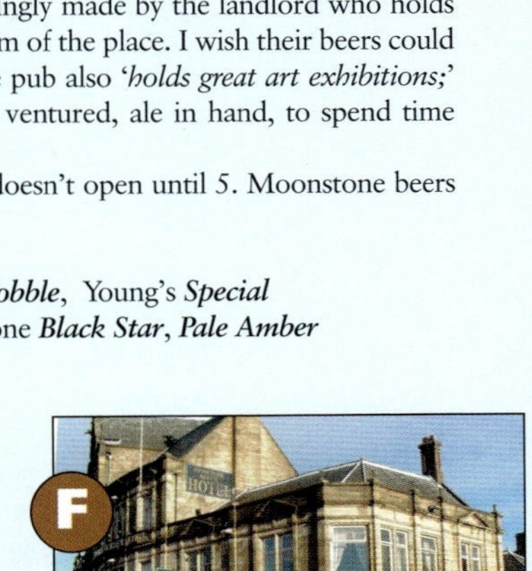

Sparrow Hawk Hotel

Church Street, BB11 2DN. Telephone 01282 421551
www.sparrowhawkhotel.co.uk
Gaffer: Jeff Mallinson
Food: Our daily menu and specials Limited menu Mon to Thu, 11.30 to 2.30, 5.to 12 Mon to Thu, 5 to 2 Fri, 11.30 to 2 Sat, 12 to 8 Sun
Separate smoking areas
Open: 11.30 to 2.30, 5 to 12 Mon to Thu, 11.30 to 2.30, 5 to 2 Fri, 11.30 to 2 Sat, 12 to 12 Sun

F

CP TV BM PG D

The Sparrow Hawk is the closest decent real ale pub to Turf Moor and on the route to the away end. Why not contact Jeff and stay at the hotel, it would make a good base for a full day spent in the town. This traditional hotel bar has a daytime student and evening local trade. It is crowded with real football fans from far and wide on a matchday. It is comfortable in the traditional beamed and carpeted hotel bar style. So it was I found relief in some Beartown ale in the corner of the main bar as the rest of the world came in for their regular meetings over ale and grub. As the Clarets say this is *'the only pub on the ground side of the ring road worth visiting.'* Andrew of Burnley says *'they do great pies; it's full of decent folk, safe and has a good atmosphere.'* Go on, book ahead, Burnley has surprised me, so too will it you.
UPDATE: The pub has special offers on cask ales on match days. The pub is unchanged throughout.

BWV 17.12.04: Beartown ***Black Bear***, E+S ***First Light***, Moorhouses ***Pendle Witches Brew***, ***Premier***, Phoenix ***Arizona***, ***1872 Porter***, ***Festive Pheasant***, Young's ***Winter Warmer***
BWV 6.6.06: Cottage ***Champflower***, Moorhouses ***Blond Witch***, ***Pendle Witches Brew***, ***Premier***, Wentworth ***Gun Park***, Woody's ***Special Bitter***, Weston's ***Old Rosie Cider***

Burnley

Burnley stands in a geological dead end, surrounded by high moors; which made it isolated and inward looking. It consists of a series of small towns on little hills, but in terms of football it has punched well above its weight. It punched well above it's weight in terms of punches as well, according to tales told by old yobbos looking at their youth through rose splattered shirt fronts.

The Leeds Liverpool Canal arrived here early, and with the hills and rain it was ideally placed for cotton manufacture. This past is being flogged in the 'Weaver's Triangle'; which Burnley claims is 'one of the best preserved Victorian landscapes in Britain.' It kept this because Burnley was too poor to attract big redevelopment bribes in the Sixties: so it can try and feed from the heritage honey pot. On a fine day we recommend a walk along the canal towards Nelson over the spectacular, mile long, embankment that is one of the engineering marvels of the Leeds-Liverpool. You can see Turf Moor on one side, and peoples' living rooms on the other.

British in India Museum

This seems to be a private museum without a website, but we would like to see what it can tell us about the Raj, and if it has any new insights on two of the most class conscious societies of recent times. We are giving the phone number so you can check opening times for yourself.
Sun Street, Colne, BB8 OJJ. 01282 613129

Cardiff

Cardiff was only made into the capital of Wales in 1955. Before that Wales had no capital city, in fact 250 years ago it hardly had a city. Before the coming of the Normans Wales was split into countless principalities, most no bigger than a council estate, and slightly less law abiding. Modern Wales grew up on the money made from coal, the food that fed the industrial revolution. The mountains that had made Wales poor also brought the best coal in Britain close to the surface, and that brought the people to Wales to mine it.

In the mid 18th Century Cardiff was a small market town, but in less than a century it had grown to be the world's biggest coal port: largely because the land and the mineral rights were owned by one family: the Bute's. This made them incredibly wealthy, but they used some of this wealth to literally build Cardiff. The docks and the entire Civic Centre, built from 1897 in a grand, but rather cold, style, was paid for by them. One of them even kicked off for Cardiff City in their first game as a professional side, in 1910!

Cardiff City centre is compact. You can easily walk between the, much banged about, Castle; the National Museum of Wales; and the Tiger Bay/docklands redevelopment. If you have a little more time we suggest a visit to the Welsh Folk Museum at St Fagans, 4 miles west of Cardiff.

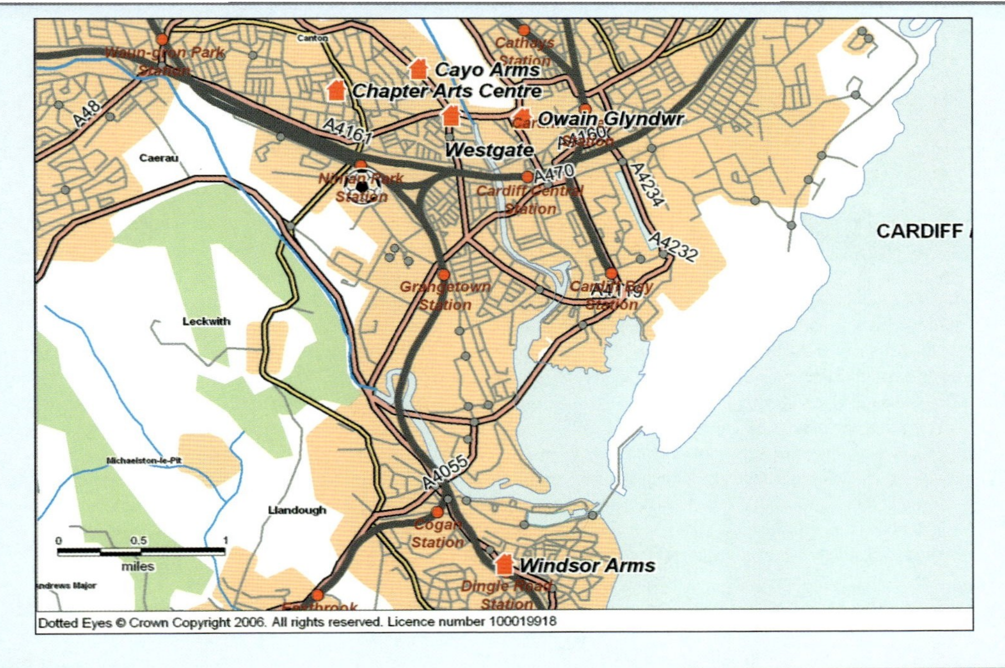

Cayo Arms

36 Cathedral Road, CF11 9LL. Telephone 02920 391910
www.cayo@celticinnspubs.co.uk
Gaffer: Nigel Sandford-Hill
Food: Seriously good-value food as seen in Cardiff good food guide
12 to 3, 5 to 9, 12 to 8 Sat
Separate smoking areas
Open: 12 to 11, 10 to 11 on big match days

F

CP SKY BM D

This hotel is a true real ale pub catering for sports fans of all types. Near Sophia Gardens, it has masses of room and easy access to all the sights of the city. Listen to rugby and cricket conversations, or chat in peaceful bliss. CAMRA Cardiff pub of the year in recent years, the pub also does accommodation and would be a great location for the full tourist bit, being just outside the town-centre in the castle area. The food comes recommended and geared towards the sort of hearty grub you want before a match. My lunch-time visit found plenty of people strolling or getting cabs from the central offices. I would love to be here the few hours before an international or during a break in a Glamorgan cricket game. Spilling into the outside areas, listening to the self-deprecating humour of Welsh sports fans is one of the joys of sporting life. *UPDATE*: The refurbishment of last February means they now have accommodation and signs that are apparently totally bi-lingual. It is now easy to recognise Nigel from the pub sign.

BWV 5.11.04: Bass ***Draught***, Brains ***Bitter***, ***Rev James***, Bullmastiff ***Son of a Bitch***, Tomos Watkin ***BB***, ***Cwrw Coroni Glyndwr***, ***OSB***
BWV 24.11.05: Brains ***Bitter***, ***Rev James***, Caledonian ***Deuchars IPA***, Fuller's ***London Pride***, Tomos Watkin ***BB***, ***Cwrw Coroni Glyndwr***, ***Merlin***, ***OSB***, Young's ***Special***

Chapter Arts Centre

Market Road, CF5 1QE Telephone 02920 311062 New
Gaffer: David Morgan
Food: Café style menu 12 to 2, 6 to 8
Non smoking
Open: 5 to 11 Mon to Thu, 5 to 12.30 Fri, 1 to 12 Sat, 4 to 10.30 Sun

The Chapter Arts Centre is exactly as described in its name but with a great range of both real ales and bottled beers to attract the discerning beer drinker. The centre houses two cinemas, a theatre and galleries, plus this excellent café bar. As expected, it is not your typical back-street pub, it is a place for those who wish to drink in an environment that is both cool and calming to their artistic senses.

David has run the bar for the last six years and has created such a reputation that the locals were keen to contact me and point out the error of my ways in last years' recommendations. The locals include the author of the recently published guide to German beers who uses the centre as his local. This may well explain the impressive bottle cabinet that stretches the bounadaries of normal pub options to global proportions. The bar itself is a classic refectory with ever changing artwork as a backdrop to the room. As the place is non-smoking, the best '*room*' for some is the enclosed courtyard which is often the place for those who like to talk of dramatic experience over a beer and fag. On Sunday nights the bar offers music in the form of a jazz band. The atmosphere is never loud even at this time. The emphasis is always on creating a place to sit and relax. The pub makes for a great alternative to the bustle of the town and lies a mere fifteen minutes walk from the ground.

BWV 2.6.06: Archers ***Champagne Charlie***, Brains ***Rev James***, Hart ***Cait-Lin***, Vale of Glamorgan ***Special Bitter***

Owain Glyndwr

10 St. Johns Road, CF10 1GL. Telephone 02920 221980
Gaffer: Glyn White
Food: Full menu, snacks, main meals and daily specials all day from 12
Separate smoking areas
Open: 11 to 11.30 Mon to Wed 11 to 1, Thu 11 to 2, Fri 11 to 4, Sun 12 to 10.30

'*Ignore your first impressions, this is not Wetherspoon's*.' The bar is sectioned and in the smaller corner bar you get the real ale. It has a mix of city professionals and students and can get very busy as regulars chase the 12 beers rotated every week. '*The pub is very female friendly*.' Tanya recommends it because '*of the fantastic choice of ales, amazing atmosphere and very pleasant work force*!' It also has an upstairs bar with resident DJ for those who wish to take advantage of the 1 o'clock licence. '*The outside drinking area is popular on big matchdays, well supervised as well*.' My visit was to the real ale section, frequented by office workers enjoying a quiet pint and shoppers looking for a restive five minutes. As Owen of Rhondda said '*you can knock em back before they knock em in, the real ales really hit the goal*'

UPDATE: Now three cask ales are served and plans for the redesign will move those ales into the main bar as the left hand bar becomes a snug.

BWV 5.11.04: Orkney ***Dark Island***, Woodforde's ***Nelsons Revenge***, Wychwood ***Hobgoblin***, Weston's ***Old Rosie*** Cider
BWV 24.11.05: Caledonian *80/-*, Camerons ***Castle Eden Ale***, Fuller's ***London Pride***

Westgate

New

49 Cowbridge Road East, CF11 9AD. Telephone 02920 303002
Gaffer: Steve Smith
Food: Good-value pub food and specials 12 to 9
Separate smoking areas
Open: 11 to 11, 11 to 12 Sat, 12 to 11.30 Sun

MP SKY BM PG D

The Westgate is my second Brains pub and it contrasts well with the Goat Major in scale and tradition. It is massive, recently redesigned in a modern pine and open-plan style and caters for the TV sports fan with big screens and ample space to stand and stare. Those sports fans are more likely to be Cardiff Blues rugby boys than City fans. The sight of the stadium just along the road is truly impressive and being on the suburban side of the bridge it will be ever-so-slightly less crowded. Eric, behind the bar, talked with fondness of the visits of fans from Ipswich, Leeds and Wolves who no doubt came to sample the Dark and chat with fellow footie fans. The locals are totally friendly, the pub proclaims it is '*proud to be your local*' and quite so. This pub was also recommended by the regulars at the Windsor for the quality of the Brains ales. I enjoyed the respite from the first winter snows in a corner of the pub, failing miserably in my attempt to understand the local dialect. I resisted the temptation to go out back and play pool with the students, rather sitting in one of the four separate drinking areas, each quite discrete in their terracotta library style. The skittle alley has now gone, as the Westgate needed more kitchen space. The Welsh food included a Welsh burger! It is, however, a pub, not a restaurant, a mix of locals' bar and town house just out of town. It makes an ideal stopping-off point in what is likely to be a crawl from the Cayo into town when the game is over.

BWV 24.11.05: Brains ***Bitter***, ***Dark***, ***Rev James***, ***SA***

Windsor Arms

93 Windsor Road, Penarth, CF64 1JF. Telephone 02920 707881
Gaffer: Clive Williams
Food: Good-value pub food from 12 to 3
Separate smoking areas
Open: 12 to 11, Wed, Fri and Sat extensions

An ale house with a restaurant attached, this pub is a real pub is for the discerning real ale drinker. The clients come from near and far via train and car to sample what is happening here. The layout offers space for groups to chat as well as those who just relax and listen. My visit was a very relaxing hour, the food looked like a bit of an institution with the regulars. The beer was a topic of conversation among small groups of professionals who had obviously chosen the pub as a comfortable haunt. All in all a top boozer that would be top of my list when I return to Cardiff. The bar is all wooden floors and barrels, loads of local community news giving it a lived-in feel that you find in the best community locals. Clive recommends using the train from Dingle Station which is less than two minutes away. Good advice as the range of ales is such that just one is a bit of a crime. *UPDATE*: Clive has taken over the ownership from Brains and the pub has been tastefully redecorated in the true Windsor Arms style. The guest ales rotate monthly.

BWV 5.11.04: Greene King ***Abbot***, ***IPA***, Hancock's ***HB***, Timothy Taylor ***Landlord***, Tomos Watkin ***Cwrw Haf***, ***OSB***
BWV 24.11.05: Brains ***Dark***, ***SA***, Brakspear ***Fire Dog***, Greene King ***Abbot***, Hancock's ***HB***, Highgate ***Fat Catz***

Need print?
We tackle everything

TLV
Expertise in Print & Design
01454 319555
TLV

TLV

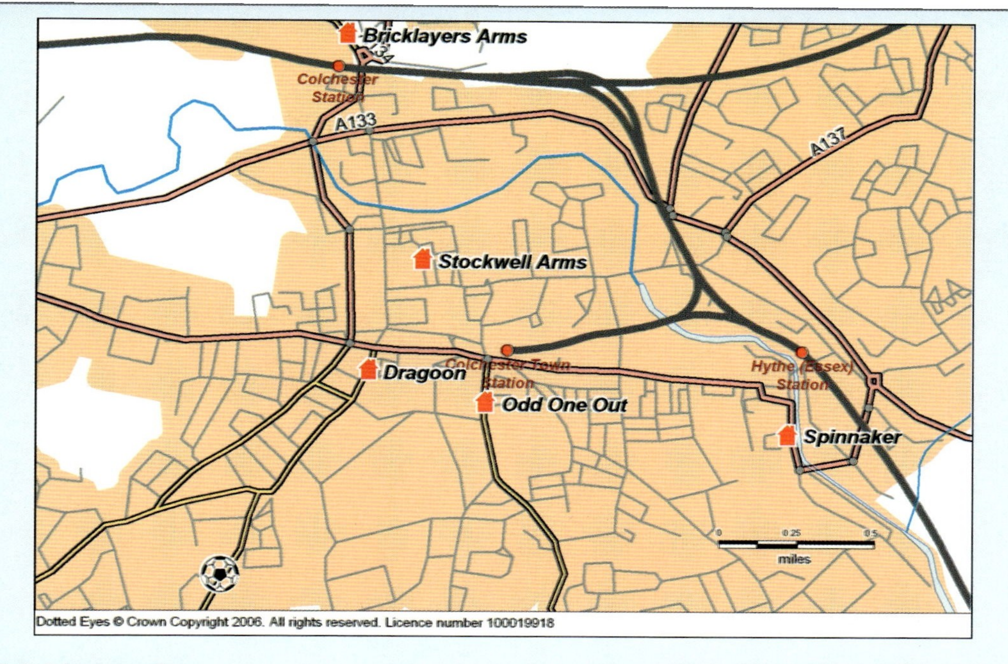

Bricklayers Arms

27 Bergholt Road, CO4 5AA. Telephone 01206 852008
Gaffer: Fred Veasey
Food: All freshly-prepared, home-cooked food. 12 to 2. No food on Sat
Separate smoking areas
Open: 11 to 3, 5.30 to 11, 11 to 12, Fri. 11 to 11 Sat. 12 to 3, 7 to 11 Sun

CP TV BM PG D

This is a cracking pub and quite a surprise given its size and initial appearance. '*It looks like one of those famous restaurant pubs that welcome children and your granny*.' The rooms are totally distinctive and the front bar would appeal to me as the sort of place to find really good mates chewing the fat over a beer and a game of pool. Being close to the station it sometimes has to close on matchdays and is so busy that food is not possible. The pub is best found via the road to the rear. This would make an ideal starting or finishing point for those who either come on the train or fancy a pint well away from the ground. They, and I, would not welcome a mass influx of away fans, but enjoy the company of real ale fans who know the difference between blind faith and loyal support. The locals are very friendly and may well join in a taxi-booking session to the ground, several miles away. The Bricklayers has regularly won CAMRA awards.
UPDATE: Bitburger lager and real ciders now feature more prominently.

BWV 18.1.06: Adnams ***Best***, ***Broadside***, ***Old Ale***, Crones ***Cider***
BWV 2.2.05: Adnams ***Bitter***, ***Broadside***, ***Old Ale***, Fuller's ***London Pride***, Timothy Taylor ***Landlord***

Dragoon

82 Butt Road, CO3 3DA. Telephone 01206 573464
Gaffer: Andy Duncan
Food: Freshly prepared and cooked menu, tailored for fans on matchdays. 11.30 to 2, 1 to 3 Sun
Smoking Throughout
Open: 11 to 11 Mon to Thu, 11 to 12 Fri, 11 to 11 Sat, 12 to 10.30 Sun

On the route from town to Layer Road, many will pass this pub without knowing of its excellence. Timber-framed with a very long bar, this is a place to sit on the many stools at that bar and chat to regular friends. They include away fans and '*homers who come from far and wide*.' My early-day visit was very different to the matchday experience, when room to sit, read and quaff quality real ale is replaced by the bubble of friends being reunited two weeks on. Ian Bown of Colchester says it well: *'You'll always get a quality pint in a friendly atmosphere along with the infamous chilli*!' The chilli served on matchdays has a legendary status, being recommended by several sources. I was perfectly content to chat with the barmaid, and then Andy, who helpfully met me on his day off. This tells you something about the welcome you will get here; nothing seems too much trouble. Despite the military insignia that surround you this is essential a townies' pub, frequented by long-standing regulars of all ages.
UPDATE: The pub is thankfully unchanged and as friendly as ever.

BWV 2.2.05: Adnams ***Bitter***, ***Old Ale***, ***Oyster Stout***
BWV 18.1.06: Adnams ***Bitter***, ***Broadside***, ***Explorer***, ***Old Ale***

Odd Man Out

28 Mersea Street, CO2 7ET. Telephone 01206 513958
Gaffer: John Parrick
Food: Nourishing cheese rolls subject to demand New
Separate smoking areas
Open: 4.30 to 11, 12 to 11 Fri, 11 to 11 Sat, 12 to 10.30 Sun

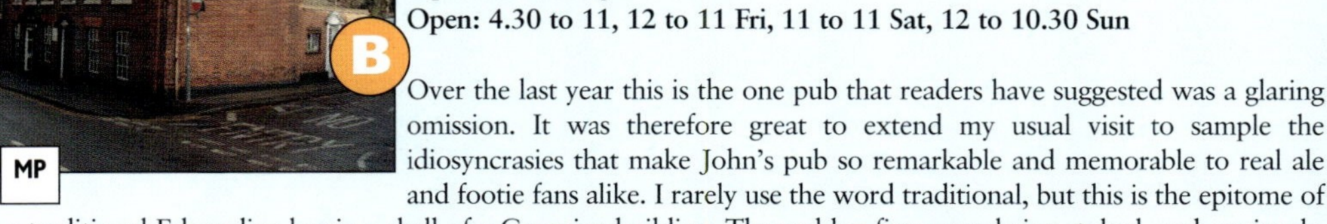

Over the last year this is the one pub that readers have suggested was a glaring omission. It was therefore great to extend my usual visit to sample the idiosyncrasies that make John's pub so remarkable and memorable to real ale and footie fans alike. I rarely use the word traditional, but this is the epitome of a traditional Edwardian bar in a shell of a Georgian building. The real log fires were being stoked, and, curiously, the paracetemol re-stocked, as I joined the early-evening drinkers in their post-work ale.

It really is a bit like being in one of those sweet shops one might find in an industrial living museum. That is not to say the pub is old-fashioned, far from it. Mobiles are requested to be turned off, there is minimal music. The chat, however, is typical of the more upwardly-mobile sections of the Colchester scene. On top of this John adds malt whiskies and real cider. There is an ever-rotating ale list that always includes a darker beer. His 20-odd years as a landlord here has resulted in the pub evolving exactly as the clientele it serves changes. As he says, at least 90% of his customers have passed at least one pub to get there. No doubt they will have travelled far because the Odd Man Out is indeed the rarity of a Colchester pub that offers a fine list of rarer ales.

BWV 18.1.06: Archers ***Best***, Nethergate ***Umbel Ale***, O'Hanlon's ***Port Stout***, Oulton ***Gone Fishing***, ***Sleet n' Snow***, Crones ***Cider***, Thatcher's ***Farmhouse***, ***Medium***, ***Ciders***

Spinnaker

Hythe Quay, CO2 8JB. Telephone 01206 793176
Gaffer: David Clayton
Food: Freshly-prepared, locally-sourced, quality pub food 2 to 2 weekdays only
Separate smoking areas
Open: 11 to 3, 5 to 11, 11 to 3, 7.30 to 11 Sat, 12 to 4, 7.30 to 10.30 Sun

This recommendation is well away from the normal footie route and therefore has something special. Not for the food – none is available on Saturdays, or for '*new age beer.*' It offers top quality beer in a pub that is simple, traditional and downright comfortable. Frequented by army colonels as well as local artisans, it is also a place to spot famous dart players. As the area around it changes, the view of the timber yards may become one of yachts and marina buildings. One hopes the pub keeps its self-proclaimed quality of being the '*cosiest pub on the quay*.' I certainly found this to be the case on my lunchtime visit. The barmaid made me very welcome and told me many a tale of the pub's qualities. The best bet is to go and see for yourself, perhaps combining a walk along the quay with a beer before the game. The masses won't like this pub, fortunately. It is definitely one for the couple or small group of genuine beer hunters looking for well kept national ales.
UPDATE: The beer continues to change regularly. Sue is still her charming self, the houses are finished and nothing much has changed at the Spinnaker.

BWV 2.2.05: Shepherd Neame ***Best***, ***Spitfire***.
BWV 18.1.06: Fuller's ***London Pride***, Greene King ***IPA***

Stockwell Arms

18 West Stockwell Street, CO1 1HN. Telephone 01206 575560 **New**
Gaffers: Brian and Shirley Jerome
Food: Good value English pub food designed to suit tourists and busy office workers,12 to 2
Smoking Throughout
Open: 11 to 11 Mon to Fri, 11 to 5, 7 to 11 Sat, 12 to 4, 7 to 10.30 Sun

When I visit a tourist location I like to find pubs that are just off the tourist trail, yet are easily-accessible to the best locations. In Colchester, the Stockwell fits the bill perfectly. Local signs will not help you find it and perhaps this explains why the pub remains as a predominantly locals' pub, where a high proportion of those visitors have discovered it for the reputation it holds for good ale and food.

What Brian doesn't know about Colchester pubs and their landlords is not worth knowing. He has been here 20-odd years and in that time the Stockwell has built a deserved reputation as the friendliest of town locals, a no-nonsense pub of the type rapidly being lost, and one that has a heart that reaches out beyond taking your money and serving ale. Brian tells me his charitable work may be less likely in the future: time takes it toll on the legs when £40,000 has been raised for charity.

Those locals range from old boys supping a pint of '*the usual*' to local town hall officers discussing the finer points of town planning. If only they could turn their thoughts to some simple maps of the town. The pub is made up of three different areas. The wings are raised and quite discrete. The central bar is the place to meet the regulars, and very friendly they were, especially when it came to directions to the next pub.

BWV 18.1.06: Caledonian ***Deuchars IPA***, Nethergate ***Augustinian***, ***Suffolk County***, ***Umbel Ale***

Colchester

Colchester was old when Boudicca led her revolt from here. It can make a great visit, but if the wind is cold, or the traffic's bad, it can feel like an enormous expanse of next to nothing. It is also a garrison town, but most of the barracks on the long walk to Layer Road are boarded up. Soon there may be so few British Army soldiers left in Britain that Luxembourg could successfully invade.

Jumbo

This ex-water tower has towered above Colchester for over 120 years. Decommissioned in the 80s, there is a fight to save it as it stands.

The Siege House

We have lots of ruins caused by bombs, but this half timbered house is the only bullet scarred building Bradwan knows of in England. The holes were made in 1648 during the Civil War.

Castle Museum

This was the biggest castle keep in Europe, and is still impressive, despite the loss of its top floors. It has a history collection, but it expensive and no effort is made to sell, or tell, you what is inside before you get to the cash desk.

Tymperleys Clock Museum

Another half timbered house. All the clocks were made in Colchester between 1640 and 1840: which suggests Colchester was chock full of clock makers; or the collector, Bernard Mason, was a bit obsessive.

If you like shellfish then Colchester open market is a place to buy.
www.colchestermuseums.org.uk

Coventry

This town, is coming like a ghost town
Ghost town, *The Specials*

Coventry is the biggest British town Bradwan has never visited, so this should be a better than average guide.

Coventry Ring Road

We know people who have claimed to have driven on the M25 without fear or loathing. We have never heard anyone say a good word for the Coventry ring road; or rather we have heard lots of good words for it, but will not write any of them down. As a website called tribalcoventry says: 'it starts from exactly nowhere and ends in you hitting a wall.'

There are nice parts within Coventry's ring road, but if you are driving you may never be able to get off it to see them: and if you are walking you have to scuttle underneath it and hope you will live to see daylight. Plenty of football clubs have been nearly driven out of existence by bad, bribe driven architecture that left empty voids and massive debts. It is probably not a comfort to realise cities have suffered the same.

The Cathedral's

One expert we talked to claimed the new building was a quid shop cathedral built down to a price, and that while Basil Spence's design is made powerful by being next to the gaunt shell of the old cathedral, it would have been poorly rated if built in another city. Having said that, the two together have had a profound effect on many we have talked to

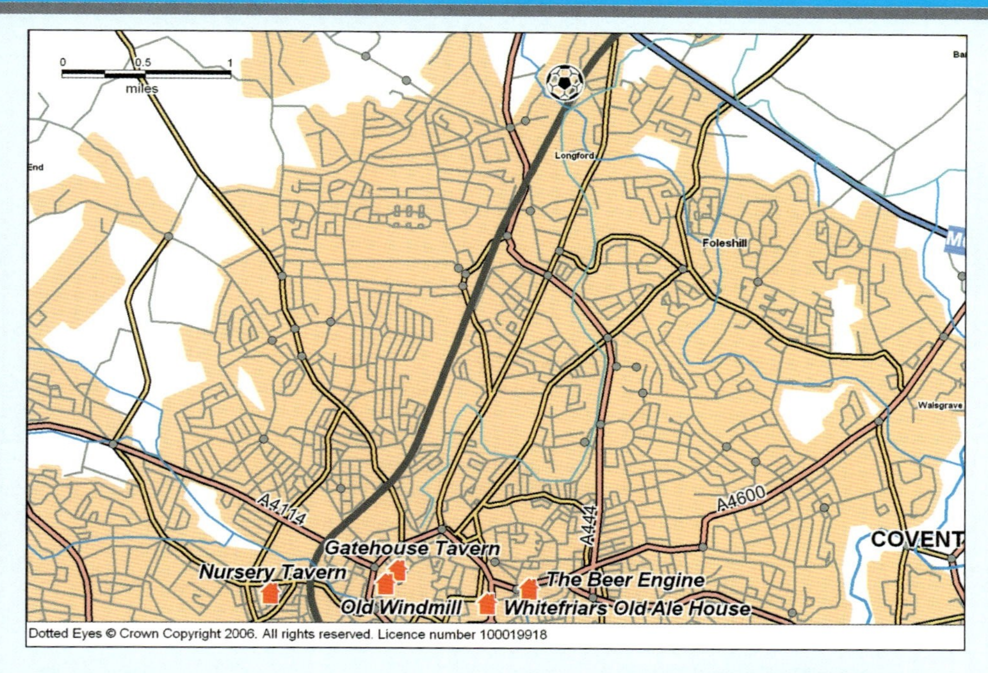

The Beer Engine

35 Far Gosford Street, CV1 5DW. Telephone 02476 267236 New
Gaffer: Ian McAllister
Food: Sunday Lunches 12 to 3
Smoking Throughout
Open: 12 to 11, 12 to 10.30 Sun

SP BM PG

The name of the pub conjures up a place where beer is everything and choice is paramount. This is so very true and demand for the ales is such that my visit found stocks low and a Wednesday beer delivery eagerly awaited. The image in my mind was confirmed when I found a pub with bare boards, plain and dark painted walls and a roaring fire, very welcome on a cold winters day.

The pub also hosts quality music sessions. They are of genuine live variety, local bands, wannabe stars and the pub suits my idea of a music pub being in the true '*cider house*' style. Then there is a total contrast at which to marvel. The walls host art collections from local artists. When I visited it was a great photograph portfolio and some framed watercolours. The regulars range from students on a night out in one of the cheaper areas to drink and more importantly eat, through discerning ale tickers, to City fans who can't quite forget their Highfield Road pub haunts. You will find that the customers are of the genuine ale type, i.e. no Carlsberg is sold, Leffe beer is the alternative of choice. The pub also has a sport all of its own that revolves around Mutley the collie who appears to own the rear of the bar. If my reporters are to be believed he is keen to play and is quite a character. My own information was gleaned by harassing Ben who wanted to light that great real fire in the best front bar.

BWV 7.3.06: Brakspear *Special*, Black Sheep *Bitter*, Marston's *Pedigree*, Tunnel *Late OTT*, *Trade Winds*

MP SKY D

Gatehouse Tavern

46 Hill Street, CY1 4AN. Telephone 02476 256796
Gaffer: Martin McKeown
Food: Good selection of main meals, freshly prepared and cooked to order 11 to 2, 6 to 9.30 Mon to Fri 11 to 3 Sat, No food Sun
Smoking Throughout
Open: 11 to 3, 5 to 11 Mon to Wed, 11 to 12 Fri and Sat, 12 to 10.30 Sun

Martin built this pub so, despite initial appearances, it only dates back to 1995. With that in mind you have to marvel at the design. It fits perfectly into my mind of a perfect beer drinking place. The scale is just right, space to stand or sit, I liken this to the very best rugby clubhouses I have visited without the language or singing associated with that genre. It offers Sky TV and is busy on all matchdays, both for rugby and the Sky Blues. It is not, however, a place for those who prefer lager. The real ale fans have a place of reverence here and as such the atmosphere is like all such pubs, i.e. more reserved than that in the city centre swilling houses. Having said that, my Sunday lunchtime was shared with the not so successful pub footie team, lagers in their hands. Someone should tell them to try some real ale, it might make a difference to the result or at least keep them on the pitch.
UPDATE: The Gatehouse has been hemmed in by redevelopments but remains a great pub with a very friendly atmosphere.

BWV 20.2.05 Church End ***Goats Milk***, ***What the Fox's Hat***, ***Classic Gold***
BWV 7.3.06: Bass ***Draught***, Church End ***Drop Goal***, Fuller's ***London Pride***

SP TV

B

Nursery Tavern

38–39 Lord Street, Chapelfields, CV5 8DA. Telephone 02476 674530
Gaffers: Harry Minten and St. John Berisford
Food: Sandwiches and chips plus Sunday lunches 12 to 2
Smoking Throughout
Open: 12 to 11.30 Mon to Thu, 11 to 12 Fri and Sat, 12 to 11 Sun

I loved the bar in which I sat. It was a shrine to Coventry and English rugby. Photos, programmes, memorabilia all set me wanting to make a foolish decision to play chase the egg just one more time. The pub is home to the VP Club 92 (*rugby supporters*) as well as the F1 Racing club. There are three rooms in all and enough choice of ale to guarantee a session for any drinker. This place is always popular, often crowded and you will never be disappointed by the friendliness of it. Add in the July garden real ale festival and the residents of Chapelfields have a local to cherish. It has all this and good pub food. It is a great street local in an area with plenty of rivalry. Now where is my gum shield?
UPDATE: Nothing has changed; it is still a brilliant locals' pub, very easy going.

BWV 20.2.05: Adnams ***Broadside***, Courage ***Best***, Greene King ***Old Speckled Hen***, Jennings ***Cumberland Ale***, John Smith's ***Cask Bitter***, Wells ***Bombardier***, York ***Yorkshire Terrier***, Thatcher's ***Heritage Cider***
BWV 7.3.06: Cottage ***Whippet Gold Cup***, Courage ***Best***, John Smith's ***Cask Bitter***, RCH ***Old Slug Porter***, Theakston's ***Dark Mild***, Wells ***Bombardier***, Wye Valley ***Hereford Pale Ale***

Old Windmill

22-23 Spon Street, CV1 3BA. Telephone 02476 252183
Gaffer: Robin Addey
Food: Good quality traditional pub food 12 to 2.30
Separate smoking areas
Open: 11 to 12, 12 to 12 Sun

Some History remains in Spon St. The post war redevelopment managed to keep the area as an island among the concrete. The Old Windmill, by its nature therefore, offers some novelty in the city. It is timber-framed, multi-roomed with flag-stoned areas as well as cosy carpeted snugs '*it is a place to take your mother in law during the day and your mistress in the evening*.' A good selection of national ales is on offer, including on this occasion Old Peculier that draws in its devotees. I would choose to return to sit in the room nearest the road, all leaded glass and bench seats and tables. From there you could enjoy a quiet lunchtime crossword and ale session. In the evening, perhaps with a group of blokes, set yourself the task of finding a pub in Coventry that has as much history in the walls and windows. The signs of refurbishment are everywhere but the essential pubbiness remains as people come and go.
UPDATE: There is an extra pump added since last year and Robin has enhanced the real ale reputation.

BWV 20.2.05 Courage ***Directors***, Ruddles ***County***, Wychwood ***Hobgoblin***, Greene King ***Old Speckled Hen***, ***IPA***, Theakston's ***Old Peculier***
BWV 7.3.06: Archers ***Golden***, Caledonian ***Deuchars IPA***, Greene King ***Old Speckled Hen***, ***Ruddles County***, Hanby ***Cherry Bank***, Theakston's ***Old Peculier***, Wychwood ***Hobgoblin***

Whitefriars Old Ale House

New

114-115 Gosford Street, CV1 5DL. Telephone 02476 251655
Gaffer: Matthew Young
Food: Good quality quick and simple food from monster breakfasts to chip butties 11 to 3
Smoking Throughout
Open: 11 to 11.30, 11 to 11 Sun

Whitefriars reopened as an ale House in 2000. Everything about the pub shouts quality and character; the building, the beers, the staff and the customers. Whitefriars is a pub from the top drawer. The pub has four different drinking areas all with odd shapes, slopes and angles plus a beer garden that hosts three beer festivals a year in April, May and August. In fact the building is so quirky that one can imagine it being quite a challenge after a few ales. Those ales are always changing, often rare and always served with enthusiasm by a team that has been here for some time and as a result looks after the beer thirsts of the customers with the care only found in the very best of real ale houses.

I really liked this pub. This was due in part to the chat I had with some new found friends from the University, too conveniently located opposite. They talked about how requests for new ales are satisfied by Paul's Monday beer searches. They also raved about the food that is simple and appropriate to a proper pub. Another unusual feature is that the pub has upstairs rooms and a separate bar there that is opened when demanded. This is often, especially at weekends when City fans return after the game, old habits die hard even when the team has moved. 6000 beers in five years is a fantastic achievement.

BWV 7.3.06: Archers ***Billy No Mates***, Greene King ***IPA***, ***Old Speckled Hen***, Oldershaw ***Alma's Brew***, Scattor Rock ***Teign Valley Tipple***, Slaughterhouse ***Black Tan***

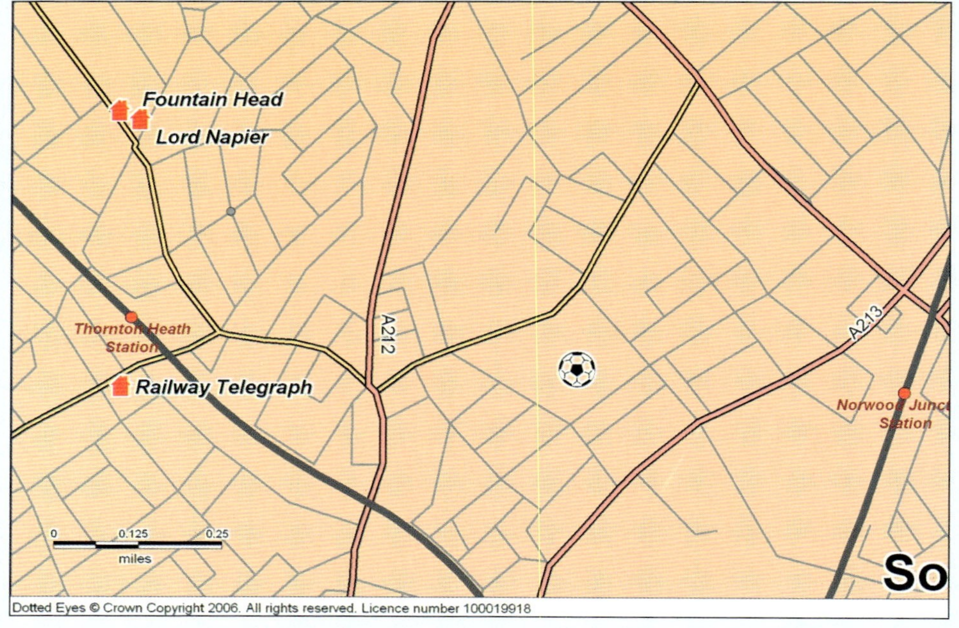

Fountain Head

114 Parchmore Road, Thornton Heath, CR7 8LX. Telephone 020 8653 4025
Gaffers: Sharon Cook and David Cox
Food: Good quality home-cooked pub food 12 to 3 New
Smoking Throughout
Open: 12 to 12, 11 to 12 Sat, 12 to 11 Sun

When one enters a pub it is often quite easy to get accurate first impressions. The first thought that came to mind on my lunchtime visit was of the word *'caring'*. It was immediately evident that the pub welcomed, and indeed encouraged, a family approach to this community pub. This approach extended to Sharon wanting the pub to be something special, very much a home from home,

The beers included the Young's seasonal ale and the pub has a distinctively roomy feel. There is one single U-shaped bar, dominated by an impressive photo of the Queen on horseback near the door. Space is certainly plentiful but no doubt the pub is often very busy, especially when the pub holds its regular quizzes, Karaoke or bingo nights. These are not themes for a modern pub but more reflect the sort of events the locals enjoy in their true local. Those regulars include fans of most London clubs, the pub will be perfectly friendly and they are used to away fans finding it on their way to, or from, the nearby Lord Napier. It is one of the obvious places to look as you leave the High Street, away from the direct route to the ground, which is 20 minutes walk away. If you were to park in the largish car park you will need to get a permit from the pub. It would also be a good choice to watch a pre match Sky game, the large screen is well used, especially when rugby internationals are staged.

BWV 22.2.06: Young's *Bitter*, *St. Georges*, *Special*

Lord Napier

111 Beulah Road, Thornton Heath, CR7 8JH. Telephone 020 8653 2286
Gaffer: Noel Fleming
Food: Sunday roast for £3.95 New
Smoking Throughout
Open: 12 to 11, 12 to 10.30 Sun

The Lord Napier is a classic Young's boozer with a fantastic twist. It claims to be '*London's best jazz pub*' and everything in the pub is geared towards fulfilling that premise. Noel has worked hard to make the pub so successful. Along with its recognition by the local CAMRA group, the inevitable has now happened and he is moving on to pastures new. No doubt, the pub will continue to be the best on offer in Thornton Heath and worth the diversion from the High Street.

The pub is at its busiest on the regular music nights. It has a resident 16 piece band that play in an impressive room that is immediately hidden behind a panelled screen in the bar. When closed the pub reverts to a Victorian classic, all glass and mirrors, chandeliers and feature windows. There is also a large Mississippi scene mural that advertises the musical heritage. I really enjoyed my lunchtime pint chatting to loyal locals. One day I would be tempted by the selection of 23 malt whiskies. On another day I would be interested to see which guests come along to jam with the smaller bands on a Thursday night. Those locals confirmed my thought that after sampling seven pubs in the Thornton Heath area, this was indeed the friendliest and had the welcome you would enjoy. Southampton fans recommended the pub to me, they will no doubt return for years; providing of course the Palace and Saints don't spoil the fun in the final game of the season, by one being promoted at the expense of the other.

BWV 22.2.06: Young's *Bitter*, *Special*

Railway Telegraph

19 Brigstock Road, Thornton Heath, CR7 7JJ. Telephone 020 8239 9857
Gaffer: Charles Bohan
Food: Kitchen under construction 12 to 2, 5 to 10 New
Separate smoking areas
Open: 12 to 2 Sun to Thu, 12 to 1am Fri and Sat

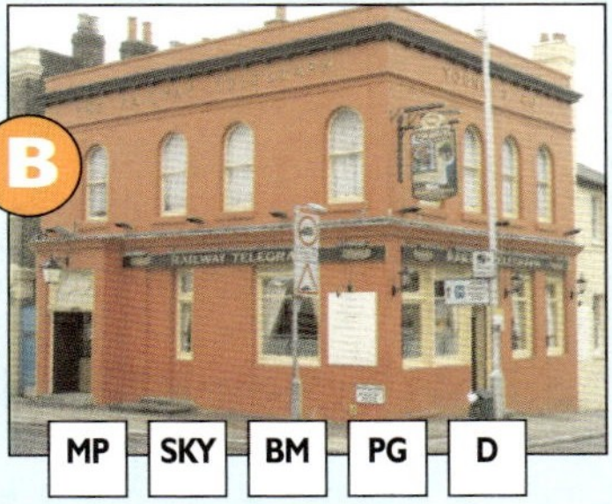

Everything about the Telegraph is impressively new. It had been recently revamped when I visited and the effect will be one that has been needed in the High Street for some time. Charles now has a pub that successfully marries both the modern and traditional. The refurbishment is not yet complete but I am assured that the new kitchens will mean good food but not to the detriment of being a good traditional pub in the classic suburban style.

The pub has very friendly staff and locals. They were very keen to talk about the beers and how this pub is really needed in the local area. There were some great features in the new design. Charles uses the stage area to crate a small snug complete with leather seats that would easily be claimed as the home of the more romantic, albeit being between the two doors to the loos. On Saturday matchdays the place buzzes. They welcome away fans who can find it very easily by looking to the right as they leave the Station. Those who wish to mix with the locals might prefer the smaller public bar area to the right of the pub. Larger groups wanting a good meeting place would enjoy the space found in the lounge area. '*Smart*' comes to mind when you gather together first impressions. It already appeals to a wide range of well heeled South Londoners. I believe this pub will be very popular in its new guise.

BWV 22.2.06: Young's ***Bitter*, *St. Georges*, *Special***

Crystal Palace

This club was named after the Crystal Palace which was moved from Hyde Park to a park 2 miles to the north of Selhurst Park. It burnt down in 1935 but the park has life size dinosaur models, a rarely open Museum, and contained the 1885 stadium that held most pre Wembley cup finals. The Crystal Palace Athletics Stadium stands on part of the site.

Dulwich is a pretty village a little further north. It is controlled by an estate, bought in 1610 by Edward Alleyn: brothel keeper, actor, controller of Royal Bears, Bulls and Mastiff Dogs, and part owner of a dog fighting pit. The estate funds Dulwich College, the school of P.G. Wodehouse. He paid homage to his school's founder by having Bertie Wooster give the false name of Eustace H. Plimsoll, The Laburnums, Alleyn Road, West Dulwich; when jailed for stealing a policemen's helmet.

The Dulwich Picture Gallery

Britain's oldest public art gallery. The collection was made for a King of Poland. He never paid for it because he stopped being King when Germany, Russia and Austria divided his country up. Sir John Soane designed the gallery; and the Sir John Soane's Museum, 13 Lincoln's Inn Fields, WC1. the best museum in Britain.
www.dulwichpicturegallery.org.uk

Croydon

Crystal Palace's town, and one that wants to be a city. The main station has always been called East Croydon, the world's most stupid station name. How are strangers supposed to know that Croydon's station begins with an E?

Derby

Years ago a member of the Bradwan staff arrived in Derby on a Sunday morning. England was not famous for excitement of a Sunday morning, but Bradwan proudly carries cultural battle honours from the grimmest of places: so our brave cultural foot soldier set off for the Cathedral for a look around and maybe catch some singing and a bit of a show. What he saw of Derby Cathedral was impressive but limited, on account of having to look through the keyhole, because the door was locked!

Derby seems to have few cultural attractions, but a few gender specific people have told us that the shops are good.

Derby Museum and Art Gallery

We like how this museum's website advertises products of Derby, rather than gibberish about 'interaction' 'education' and 'multi-culturalism'. What is the point of a town museum that does not proudly boast about the town and culture that built it? Ignoring that is not multi-culturalism, it is death-to-culturalism.

Derby Museum has the world's best display of Crown Derby china, amongst the finest practical and pleasing of human artifacts. It also boasts the largest collections of paintings by Joseph Wright (1734-97). In terms of originality in the use of light, colour and form and he predates, and ranks with, Turner. He was the first successful English artist to live outside London; still stands as one of our greatest northern painters; and was amongst the first to paint scientific and industrial scenes.

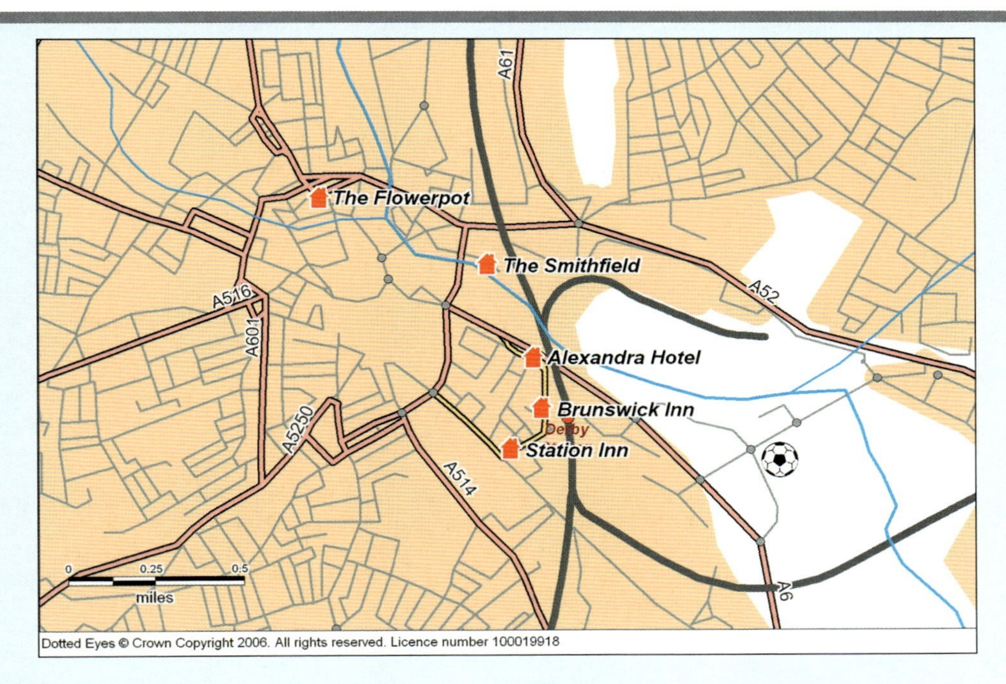

Alexandra Hotel

203 Siddals Road, DE1 2QE. Telephone 01332 293993
Gaffer: Mark Robbins
Food: Simple traditional food from 11
Separate smoking areas
Open: 11 to 11, 12 to 3, 7 to 10.30 Sun

CP BM D

This railway picture (well, DMU) decorated ale house is a two-bar traditional style pub. Mark gives a friendly Derby welcome to lovers of railways and real ale. My visit was all the more pleasant because of the regularity that real ale fans arrived from the station carrying their CAMRA guides, living the real ale tickers' dream. Filled by the humour on the walls and from the greeting, I would leave my real ale ticking mentality on the train, and just enjoy the ale. You will not find a better choice of micro-brews and the pub is well used to people travelling between it and its near neighbour. This pub is always busy on matchdays and has a loyal fan base of Rams from well beyond Derby. It also has an impressive list of imported beers.
UPDATE: There are 8/9 ales at the weekend, my visit was midweek.

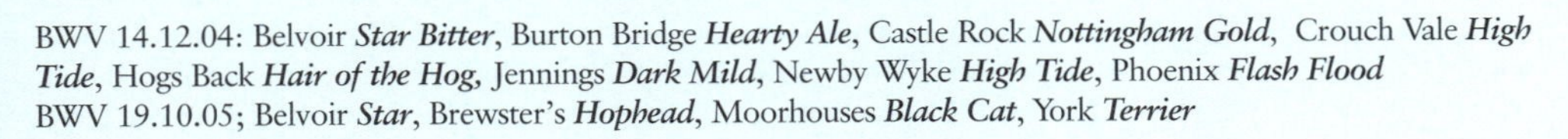

BWV 14.12.04: Belvoir ***Star Bitter***, Burton Bridge ***Hearty Ale***, Castle Rock ***Nottingham Gold***, Crouch Vale ***High Tide***, Hogs Back ***Hair of the Hog,*** Jennings ***Dark Mild***, Newby Wyke ***High Tide***, Phoenix ***Flash Flood***
BWV 19.10.05; Belvoir ***Star***, Brewster's ***Hophead***, Moorhouses ***Black Cat***, York ***Terrier***

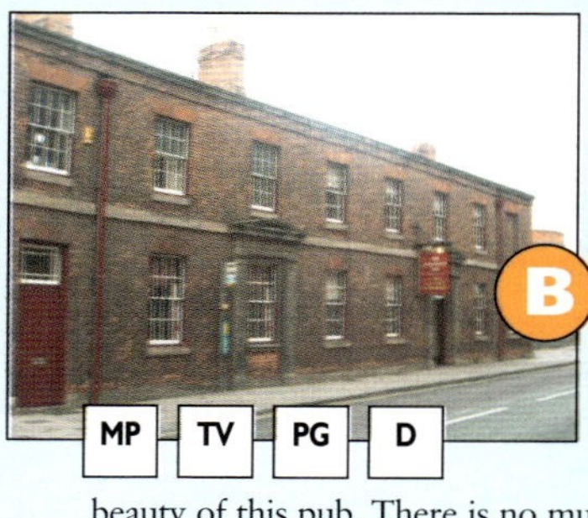

Brunswick Inn

1 Railway Terrace, DE1 2RU. Telephone 01332 290677
Gaffer: Graham Yates
Food: Good home-made pub grub all day from 12
Separate smoking areas
Open: 11 to 11

Yes, an Everards-owned pub, yet with its own brewery. It is delicious (change to any superlative here). Six in-house brews and up to 10 others mean that you will find something to suit all tastes here. The Brunswick ales always include a mild and a wide range of strengths. The distinctive triangular building adds to the beauty of this pub. There is no music and food is only available upstairs on matchdays as it is always busy, '*This is Derby's best pub* (*If not the World's*)' (Anon) and also one of my most-recommended pubs over the last year. Obviously, Graham is doing something special here. The groups who meet here are pretty diverse as well, including political parties, footie fans and a beer-drinking knitting club. The variety of rooms becomes particularly useful on these occasions. The number of awards is massive, including regional pub of the year.

BWV 14.12.04: Brunswick ***Rambo***, ***Black Trout***, ***Railway Porter***, ***Triple Hop***, ***Mild***, Holden's ***Golden***, Everards ***Sleigh Bell***, Timothy Taylor ***Landlord***, 3 Rivers ***Old Disreputable***, Weston's ***Old Rosie Cider***
BWV 19.10.05: Badger ***Tanglefoot***, Beartown ***Wheat Beer***, Brunswick ***Bitter***, ***Father Mike's Dark Rich Ruby Mild***, ***Railway Porter***, ***Triple Gold***, ***Triple Hop***, Everards ***Beacon***, ***Equinox***, Halifax ***Rhode Island Red***, Marston's ***Pedigree***, Timothy Taylor ***Landlord***, Weston's ***Old Rosie Cider***

The Flowerpot

25 King Street, DE1 3DZ. Telephone 01332 204955 **New**
Gaffer: Sylvia Manners
Food: Quality home-made English food with daily specials
12 to 2.30 Mon to Wed, 12 to 6.30 Thu to Sat, 12 to 5.30 Sun
Smoking Throughout (cellar non-smoking 12 to 2 Mon to Fri)
Open: 11 to 11, Mon to Thu, 11 to 12 Fri and Sat, 11 to 11 Sun

Sometimes it takes a while to realise one is falling in love. A year on from my first visit and the Flowerpot has had this effect on me. It is the pub itself that has turned my head from the Alex and Brunswick for a while. A stroll along the Derwent and then in to the town found me spending a couple of hours swooning over the design, the ales and the simplicity of this great town ale-house.

Paul, a regular, described it as '*the best pub, with the best beer, top quality with a quality repartee*'. It is a place for conversation, for quiet contemplation, and has a buzz of contentment during the day. The Flowerpot is the pub where students take their parents for lunch, '*they can get mother's home cooked food*' here. It has quality music, yet is not a student pub. I wondered with a nostalgic glow about the forthcoming appearances of Dr. Feelgood and The Climax Blues Band, as well as the regular tribute band sessions. These gigs are held in the carefully designed cellar, which has a separate entrance that allows the other main bar to continue serving regulars ale-heads in relatively peaceful harmony. The pub offers 15 different ales at any one time and also has rotating cider and Perry.

BWV 25.10.05: Acorn ***Summer Pale***, Archers ***Harvest Ale***, Bradfield ***Jack O'Lantern***, Greene King ***Abbot***, Hartington ***Bitter***, ***IPA***, Hook Norton ***Best Bitter***, Kelham Island ***Pale Rider***, Marston's ***Pedigree***, Newby Wyke ***Scooby Doo***, Salamander ***Bette Noir***, Whim ***Arbour Light***, Strawberry Fields ***Cider***

The Smithfield

New

Meadow Road, DE1 2BH. Telephone 01332 370429
www.smithfield.co.uk
Gaffers: Roger and Penny Myring
Food: Rolls at bars on match-days
Smoking Throughout
Open: 11 to 11

CP JB

As promised to my recommenders, the Smithfield is a must-visit entry to the guide. On the River Derwent, the Smithfield has a great location for walking out to the ground, and also for having a bit of exclusivity from the town pubbers and clubbers. Roger and Penny run a great pub which is very much a locals' and regulars' hostelry that welcomes visitors searching out their particular niche in the real ale scene. They specialise in the style of ales popularised by Oakham ales, i.e. paler ales that suit their particular tastes.

Roger, who is a season ticket holder, says it is 18 minutes from pub to seat. On matchdays it will be very busy and very friendly, the best days being when the garden can be used. The pub itself, however, is brilliant at any time. The three separate bars include a games room that doubles as a place for families to seat children. I enjoyed the main bar with caricatures of the team members (*pub team, not Rams*). The quadrant shape of the building just adds to its quirkiness. It was advertising a Blues, Booze, and Barbecue event, and the regulars assured me that at these type of events you see Penny at her bubbly best. A top pub indeed, thanks for the recommendation chaps. The banner proclaims the Smithfield as local CAMRA pub of the year 2003.

BWV 19.10.05: Bass ***Draught***, Burton Bridge ***Top Dog Stout***, Hartington ***IPA***, Hook Norton ***Old Hooky***, Hop Back ***Crop Circle***, Oakham ***Bishops Farewell***, ***JHB***, ***White Dwarf***

Station Inn

12 Midland Road, DE1 2SN. Telephone 01332 608014
Gaffer: Dave Lalor
Smoking Throughout
Open: 12 to 2.30, 5 to 12

MP TV JB D

I sometimes want quality more than quantity, so this fits the bill perfectly. Dave serves fantastic ale including Bass from the jug. The locals have a sporting prowess, the pub being a magnet for local sporting personalities and teams in town. It is also well worth checking out the function room at the rear with its massive mirror. This is the place to start the Derby crawl. As I found out, it is a pub with all the trimmings with a style that so often is lost as city centres get gentrified. The pub has a pool table but it is usually too crowded on matchdays for it to be used. Dave has made a great effort to introduce real ale to the pub and deserves the support that is found in the local area. It will always be part of my mini-crawl. The locals are very friendly and likely to be genuine residents with all the qualities you want to find when visiting a town for the first time.

UPDATE: Guest ales increase at weekends. Best-kept cellar award

BWV 14.12.04: Bass ***Draught***, Black Sheep ***Bitter***, Caledonian ***Deuchars IPA***
BWV 14.12.05: Bass ***Draught***, Caledonian ***Deuchars IPA***

This page gives one taxi company in each town. There is no recommendation as to their reliability. They are taken from random internet searches for taxis in the town and then chosen by these criteria:

- I may have used them on my travels. I usually ask a landlord to recommend a cab company
- Based in the town centre or near the station
- Large enough to be able to afford advertising nationally
- The first I came across if the above are not immediately found

I know this is a bit subjective but I often suggest getting a taxi to the ground so it would be remiss of me not to offer some numbers.

	Taxi	Number
BARNSLEY	Premier	01226 295555
BIRMINGHAM	Silverline	01217 666336
BURNLEY	Kings	01282 433566
CARDIFF	Castle	02920 344344
COLCHESTER	Town	01206 515151
COVENTRY	Central	02476 333333
CRYSTAL PALACE	Z cars	02086 832345
DERBY	Star	01332 292020
HULL	Apple	01482 226343
IPSWICH	Embassy	01473 258888
LEEDS	Seacroft	01132 930434
LEICESTER	Quick	01162 412662
LUTON	Chiltern	01582 737373
NORWICH	Gold star	01603 488888
PLYMOUTH	Union	01752 302010
PRESTON	Guild	01772 563003
QPR	Delta	02085 307181
SHEFFIELD WEDNESDAY	Mercury	01142 662662
SOUTHAMPTON	Radio	02380 666666
SOUTHEND	Associated	01702 611611
STOKE	Five towns	01782 266266
SUNDERLAND	Town End	01915 160025
WEST BROM	Kingswood	01923 662233
WOLVERHAMPTON	Wilfruna	01902 332500

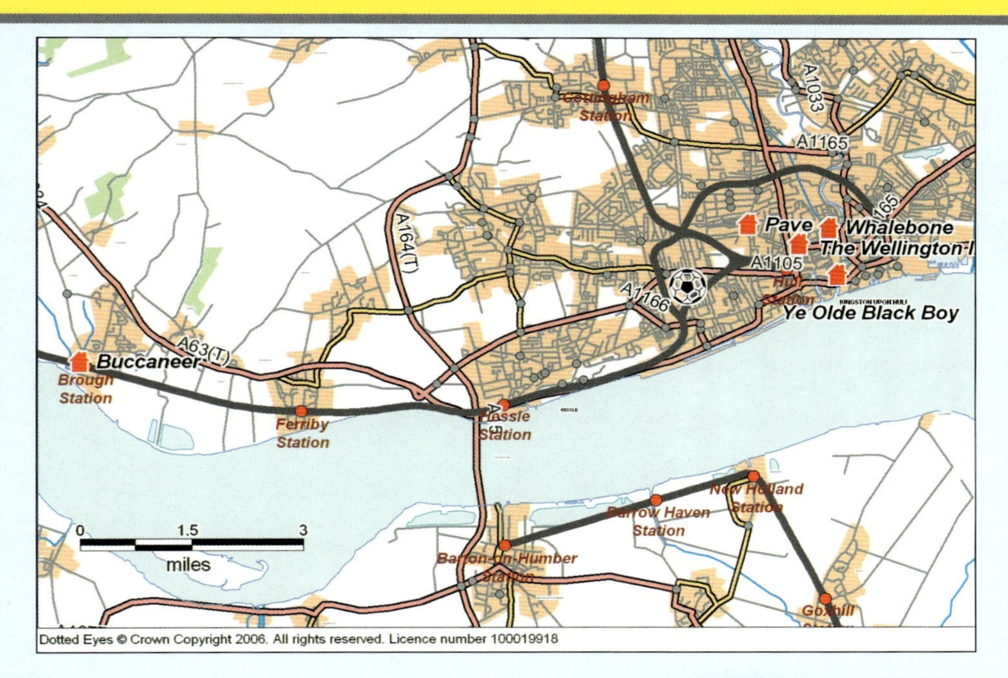

Buccaneer

47 Station Road, Brough, HU15 1DZ. Telephone 01842 667435
Gaffer: Rob Johnson
Food: Excellent, good value, all home-cooked menu 12 to 2, 6 to 9
Separate smoking areas
Open: 12 to 11

CP BM

The Buccaneer is a large, comfortable station hotel-style pub in a village that has good rail access to Hull. Its history, however, predates the railway and it is well worth chatting to the locals to find connections with the crossing of the river, local aeroplane manufacture and Dick Turpin. *'Trains leave regularly from the nearby station directly into Hull city centre.'* With this in mind it offers a good alternative to the drag of parking in the city centre. This pub is for those who wish to avoid the crowds yet get good ale served to discerning locals. The food is important here so I would recommend this to those who wish to eat well, rather than chance footie food. Have a leisurely lunch and *'let the train take the strain.'* My visit found one such lunchtime session in full flow, regulars sipping their usual, married couples out with parents for lunch and the local lads and ladettes in full banter about national footie events. All was very country village localish.
UPDATE: This pub is at its best when small groups meet up with the locals on a matchday. They are made very welcome. The pub may well have accommodation later in the season.

BWV 15.10.04: Black Sheep ***Bitter***, Tetley's ***Cask Bitter***
BWV 26.1.05: Bass ***Draught***, Black Sheep ***Bitter***, Tetley's ***Cask Bitter***, ***Dark Mild***

Pave

New

16-20 Princes Avenue, HU5 3QA. Telephone 01482 333181
Gaffer: Steve Shaw
Food: Menu that ranges from tapas, through pasta to steaks; all home-cooked in café bar style 11 to 7 Tue to Sat, 12 to 7 Sun and Mon
Smoking Throughout
Open: 11 to 11 Sun to Thu, 11 to 11.30 Fri and Sat

The pubs in Hull seem reluctant to offer food, and so for the service of those who like a good bite to eat, I recommend the Pave. It stands it own as a great ale house as well as a stylish street-pavement bar. The descriptors that come to mind are many and varied. Chic, relaxed, trendy, are often clichés but the Pave really goes the extra mile to create the ambiance that is appreciated by a growing number of the middle-incomed residents of Humberside.

The bar has a distinctively European feel that includes great pavement tables and a choice of bottled and draught world beers. I would not be surprised to see tables being waited-on, perhaps the Saturday door-man might do so during the week! The background tone is set by jazz played at a level that encourages romantic conversation, should that be your want, or allows real conversation over the ales selected from both fine nationals and Yorkshire independent brewers. It deserves to be very busy on most days, especially when families and children come for a pre-match meal. The pub has only been open for four years, again setting a trend. It was previously three shops that have been converted to a large single bar with massive picture windows that look out onto Princes Avenue, from which the name is created. This is definitely a no colours or caps pub. Who would want to anyway?

BWV 26.1.06: Caledonian ***Deuchars IPA***, Copper Dragon ***Best Bitter***, Theakston's ***Best***, ***XB***

The Wellington Inn

55 Russell Street, HU2 9AB. Telephone 01482 329486
Gaffer: Richard Gant
Separate smoking areas
Open: 12 to 11

The Welly comes to this guide courtesy of recommendations from fans and Alex at the Whalebone, and in doing so provides a useful halfway point for those making the trek from his pub to the ground. It is, however, a great pub in its own right and would be worthy of an entry because of the quality of ales on offer and because it has a great location just off Freetown Way.

Those ales are supplemented by European beers and great ciders. The number increases to nine at weekends. The pub is a classic street-corner local which has been reborn since Janette and Richard moved here from the Olde Black Boy two years ago. In doing so they brought a real ale light to this previously tired pub. The design of the pub means light is an issue. As time moves on the large curtains need to be drawn and redrawn, much to the amusement of this weary visitor. My lunch-time visit found the company of Pete, a great host, and Kevin and Dave. Dave was quick to compliment the staff being '*not from central casting, but friendly and efficient*'. Kevin described his fellow drinkers as '*a bunch with eclectic, maybe catholic tastes.*' That was certainly true of Pete's iPod selections. I would defy anyone to recognise the music in the background. The pub is rightly very popular on the real ale scene, being particularly busy on both Association and League match-days. They would love away fans to find it more regularly. It will certainly be a great choice.

BWV 26.1.06: Copper Dragon ***Black Gold***, Hambleton ***Bitter***, Tetley's ***Cask Bitter***, Timothy Taylor ***Landlord***,

Whalebone

165 Wincolmlee, HU2 OPA. Telephone 01842 327980
Gaffer: Alex Craig
Smoking Throughout
Open: 11 to 12

B

MP SKY BM PG

This is a horseshoe-shaped bar, sandwiched between two roads and the Whalebone brewery. *'It is like a museum of riverside Hull life.'* The bottles and beer mats on show testify to its popularity. Images of rugby league, as well as Tigers past, give this a traditional sporty feel. Park up and get a taxi to this pub if you want to try the extensive range of brews. It will be well worth it because the Whalebone ales are something a bit special especially if, like me, you appreciate darker beers. I settled into a corner, watched rugby league on the TV and soon found a great friendship, both among the locals and bar staff. The characters here are really that, i.e. ready to talk and tell you of their glorious sporting heritage. There was a temptation to stay here all evening. If I had to choose only one pub in Hull, this would be it; I fell in love with the place and its comfort.
UPDATE: The Whalebone has been well used over the year and is proving as brilliant to readers as I found it last year.

BWV 15.10.04: Hart ***Amber***, Timothy Taylor ***Landlord***, Tom Wood ***Best Bitter***, Whalebone ***Neck Oil***, ***Mild***, Kingston ***Black Cider***, Weston's ***Old Rosie***
BWV 26.1.06: Rudgate ***Mount Hood***, Timothy Taylor ***Landlord***, Tom Wood ***Best Bitter***, Whalebone ***Diana Mild***, ***Full Ship***, ***Neck Oil Bitter***, KB ***Strong Dry Cider***, Weston's ***Old Rosie***

Ye Olde Black Boy

150 High Street, HU1 1PS. Telephone 01482 326516
Gaffer: Alan Murphy
Smoking Throughout
Open: 12 to 11

MP TV BM PG

This is a two bar wooden-panelled and pew style pub that has tin-plate posters and breweriana to add interest. Not that you will get to see them as it gets so busy it becomes standing room only for most evenings and especially on matchdays. The Olde Black Boy, which wins regular CAMRA awards for the quality and range of ales, is unusual in central Hull. It also attracts tourists who love the back alley, yet high street, location, away from the masses of shoppers or club hunters. *'It has a reputation of being haunted although it would rarely be quiet enough to test that assertion.'* This dimly-lit pub has the smell of snuff/ready rub that adds to its charm. Space can be found when people move on. The atmosphere is very friendly, the clientele being varied in age, but not in their love of a great pub. On my visit many were choosing to use the extra upstairs rooms.
UPDATE: Food is no longer available. Six real ales are available at week-ends. Folk music takes place on Monday nights.

BWV 15.10.04: Arundel *Leaky Willie*, Exmoor *Wildcat*, Gale's *Trafalgar*, Nethergate *Monks Habit*, York Brewery *Ghost Ale*
BWV 26.1.06: Caledonian *Deuchars IPA*, Copper Dragon *Golden Pippin*, Jennings *Cumberland Ale*, Rooster's *Yankee*, Springhead *Roaring Meg*

Hull

The King's Town on the Hull River had one of the largest royal armouries in England. In 1643 Charles I came for 'his' weapons, but Hull locked the town gates and soon after, the Civil War started. Kingston upon Hull's defiance is seen by some as showing independence of spirit and thought. Others claim it shows Hull has a fondness for weapons and locking the gates against outsiders. However Bradwan likes Hull. The city centre can feel clean and prosperous, almost Dutch on a bright day.

The High Street

This has a golden statue of King Billy (William III) and the fish market at the bottom, Blackboys half way up, and a set of good museums just beyond. The best exhibit was a Scud missile sized Ancient British dugout boat. It is now displayed in a case with poor light: which was probably done as a mistake, or to hide the fact that the conservation did not work well.

The Humber

The riverside shows one of our most dramatic urban riverscapes. The great width, the Humber Bridge, and the Lincolnshire bank frame a massive sky, best seen from the old ferry pier. If you are a gentleman you can then visit one of the UK's finest Gents. Shining cooper and brass remind us of days when councils spent money; gave a service; and built things to be proud of. Now you get one of the three. Hull is one of the few towns that have free public toilets, let alone clean ones.

Ipswich

Bradwan has not been to Ipswich for ages, and the Borough Council web site freezes the computer when we try to visit: still, we believe that seeing a place only produces prejudice. Suffolk is a pretty county, and is geographically surprisingly varied. It was also very wealthy in the Middle Ages, so there are plenty of expensive churches worth seeing. We do not know why forward looking Ipswich is only a town, despite being given a charter by King John in 1200, while Norwich, its slightly more rural neighbour, has always been a city. You are best off not seeking answers to this question in an Ipswich pub on a match day though.

Ipswich is a very pleasant town to stroll around. There are some interesting late medieval buildings and a good town museum, which has Saxon weapons and jewellery, and replicas of the Sutton Hoo and Mildenhall treasures, which were found nearby but shipped off to the British Museum in London.

Cardinal Wolsey was born in Ipswich. He was a commoner who became Henry VIII's Chancellor. He started building a big, impressive college in Ipswich, but when he failed to get Henry VIII a divorce a long list of claimed abuses and corruption in office was used to unseat him. Like many football clubs, and he certainly would have bought one if he was alive today, his college's finances were just a fog of lies, and just a gateway stands as the sole memorial to vain ambition.

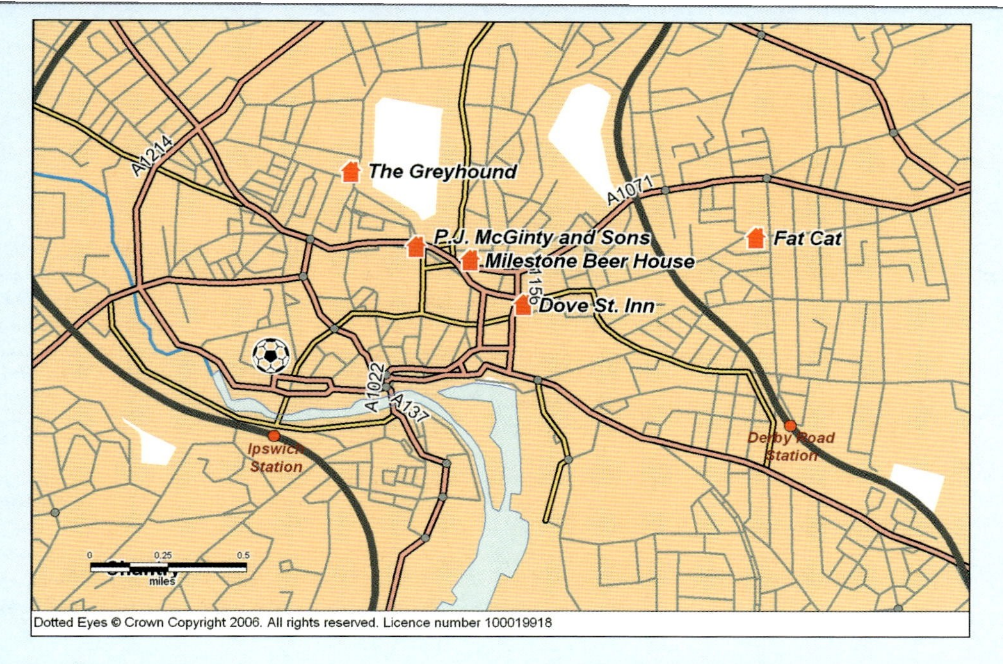

Dove Street Inn

76 St. Helens Street, IP4 2LA. Telephone 01473 211270
Gaffer: Ady Smith
Food: Pub grub, e.g. chilli, curry, beef and ale soup 12 to 12, 12 to 11 Sun
Smoking Throughout – Open: 12 to 12, 12 to 11 Sun

B

CP TV BM PG D

Ady runs this top boozer and has great plans to make it even better. It has '*excellent beer, hearty food and is 15 minutes stomp from Portman Road.*' This is a light, clean and airy pub with wooden floors and ever-changing guest ales. It also specialises in Belgian beers, Birra Moretti and numerous bottled ales. If you have tried the Milestone then you will love this – it has more of an ale emphasis than food. However, Slim Shaney comments how the '*top hot-pot tops the lot pre-match.*' And '*the landlady has great baps over which you can conduct a post-match mortem.*'
UPDATE: Evening Standard awards, the new tap room, an extension to the rear to come? The Dove now leads the way in the town centre. Ady will soon be concentrating all his time here.

BWV 21.9.04: Adnams ***Explorer***, Crouch Vale ***Brewers Gold***, Fuller's ***London Pride***, Greene King ***IPA***, Mauldons ***Summer Gold***, Nethergate ***Umbel Ale***, Oakham ***JHB***, Outlaw ***Jerry's Aromatic Lager***, Stonehenge ***Danish Dynamite***, ***Wolf Bitter***
BWV 18.1.06: Adnams ***Broadside***, Crouch Vale ***Brewers Gold***, ***Happy Santa***, Elgood's ***Golden Newt***, North Brink ***Porter***, Everards ***Tiger***, Exmoor ***Ale***, Fuller's ***London Pride***, Green Jack ***Cherry Popper***, ***Professor Plumb***, Mauldons ***Dickens***, ***MicCawber's Mild***, Mighty Oak ***Bingle Jells***, ***Oscar Wilde Mild***, Saxon ***Strong***, Nethergate ***Umbel Ale***, Theakston's ***Old Peculier***, Timothy Taylor ***Landlord***, Woodforde's ***Wherry***, ***Broad Oak***, ***New Forest***, ***Saxon***, Weston's ***Ciders***

Fat Cat

288 Spring Road, IP4 5NL. Telephone 01473 726524
Gaffer: John Keatley
Food: Home made pies, pasties and rolls
Smoking Throughout
Open: 12 to 11, 11 to 11 Sat, 12 to 10.30 Sun

With wooden floors and panelling, and light and airy, this pub offers comfort for all shapes of beer drinker. The larger area is great for just standing and chatting while smaller groups can hide behind walls. You could spend all day just people-watching here. It is described as having '*a beer festival every day in this classic Victorian boozer.*' The name Fat Cat will tell most people who read this that the quality is so good it is difficult to describe without being too gushing. As local Neil Garrod says '*It is a fantastic real ale pub that welcomes well-behaved away fans.*' The fame as a friendly footie pub is legendary among those who have shared taxis to the ground, this Ipswich moggie is truly the cat's whiskers.
UPDATE: Fat Cat own brews are now a regular feature in this great pub that remains very popular.

BWV 21.9.04: Crouch Vale ***Brewers Gold,*** Freeminer ***Speculation***, Fuller's ***London Pride***, Hop Back ***Summer Lightning***, Kent ***Boudicca Strong***, Mighty Oak ***Oscar Wilde Mild***, ***Simply The Best***, Oakham ***JHB***, Otter ***Beautiful Daze***, ***St Peter's Organic***
BWV 19.1.06: Adnams ***Bitter***, Crouch Vale ***Brewers Gold***, Fat Cat ***Bitter***, ***Hangover***, ***Top Cat***, Fuller's ***London Pride***, Kent ***Ported Porter***, Moles ***Best***, Oakham ***Black Hole Porter***, Oulton ***Mudford Mild***, ***Wet and Windy***, St. Austell ***Tribute***, Shepherd Neame ***Spitfire***, Wells ***Bombardier***, Woodforde's ***Great Eastern***, ***Wherry***, Young's ***Bitter***

The Greyhound

9 Henley Road, IP1 3SE. Telephone 01473 752862 **New**
Gaffer: Nigel Paul
Food: Home-made bar food menu that is altered to suit fans on match-days 12 to 2, 5 to 9
Smoking Throughout
Open: 11 to 2.30, 5 to 11 Mon to Fri, 11 to 11 Sat, 12 to 10.30 Sun

The Greyhound is in the leafy Christchurch Park area of town and among the large mansions and flats that provide plenty of the chattering classes as customers. Thus my visit on a wet Wednesday evening found this great pub very busy early evening, with the conversations ranging from non-league teams to the state of the Iraq war. What impressed me most was the number of father and son groups, along with pairs of women, comfortably eating out in what is their regular local.

The pub has two entrances. The smaller snug was a perfect retreat from the gentle bustle of the larger, brighter distressed-style lounge. The décor doesn't need any gimmicks; it is simple, warm and comfortable without the need either for large settees so often found when pubs choose this style of design. In reality that is what makes this pub stand out for me. It could easily drift into false pretensions but Nigel has created a great real pub, for real people to drink quality ale and eat great food. If you want some variety to the others in this guide, i.e. fewer ales but certain quality, then the walk up the hill from town makes it a great starting point. As one new found friend said, you get all that and '*top tottie as well*'.

BWV 18.1.06: Adnams ***Bitter***, ***Broadside***, ***Explorer***, ***Fisherman***, Timothy Taylor ***Landlord***

P.J. McGinty and Sons

New

15 Northgate Street, IP1 3BY. Telephone 01473 251515
Gaffer: Shane O'Toole
Food: Thai Restaurant attached to the pub 11 to 11
Smoking Throughout
Open: 11 to 11, 11 to 12 Fri and Sat

Such was my frustration with walking within the inner ring road, looking for a pub that wasn't subject to the police insistence on no away fans, that I have here an entry that will be somewhat controversial. This is my one and only classic Irish pub and my recommendation is to come in for the Guinness rather than try and search in vain in town. The masses of away fans will have been herded into the Station Hotel or a nearby lager bar. Those who escape might find Manning's and their resident Saturday chavs. Those who are crawling through my entries will see McGinty's on the route from the Greyhound to the Milestone and therefore, why not pop in to catch up on the live Sky game.

The pub has a great reputation for its friendliness, born out of the enthusiasm of the now departed former landlord, Michael Collins. The pub will perhaps be full of their own resident rugby types and it will not take long for you to be drawn into conversation or, in an evening session, typical drinking fun and games. The pub is a split-level bar, draped in Irish memorabilia. Shane, the new boss, has his own heritage that is genuinely Celtic, albeit via the Midlands en route. Last year, this was my location to watch England play on TV before returning to a marathon session at the Dove. There is real ale on offer and Shane plans to extend the choice, but I ignored this because when in Rome…

BWV 18.1.07: Adnams ***Broadside***, Greene King ***IPA***

Milestone Beer House

5 Woodbridge Road, IP4 2EA. Telephone 01473 252425
Gaffer: Ady Smith
Food: Wholesome pub grub 12 to 2, 5 to 9, 12 to 2, 5 to 7 Fri and Sat, 12 to 7 Sun
Smoking Throughout
Open: 12 to 2.30, 5 to 11 Mon to Thu, 12 to 11 Fri and Sat, 12 to 10.30 Sun

The Milestone was the Evening Standard pub of the year and its reputation has spread well beyond Ipswich. My visit was on the night of an England friendly, no Sky TV and is all the better for it. Unpretentious, clean and comfortable, it has diversions in traditional pub pool and darts, good food and above all good knowledgeable service. '*Make sure you check the ale board before ordering, you might miss a rarity. It is the only place for top ale and good live music.*' Ady and his staff have created a great pub of rare town quality.
UPDATE: Changes are on the way as Ady moves on. The beer and music remains good.

BWV 2.5.05: Adnams ***Bitter***, Badger ***Slurpin Snowman***, Bateman ***Hopbine Bitter***, Brains ***SA***, Caledonian ***Deuchars IPA***, ***Haggis Bash Bitter***, Fuller's ***London Pride***, Greene King ***Abbot***, ***IPA***, ***Old Speckled Hen***, Hop Back ***GFB***, ***Summer Lightning***, Nethergate ***Umbel Ale***, Mauldons ***Miles Better***, ***Black Adder***, Phoenix ***Snowbound***, Broad Oak Moonshine ***Cider***, Weston's ***Old Rosie Cider***
BWV 18.1.06: Adnams ***Broadside***, Bateman ***Dark Mild***, Black Country ***BFG***, Brain's ***Mild***, Grainstore ***Steamin' Billy***, Hook Norton ***303 AD***, Mauldons ***Eatanswill Old***, Young's ***Winter Warmer***

The winner of the competition was Malcolm Claringbold. His entry into the competition was made over a lunchtime session with Mally and his Carlisle supporting mates in the Inn on The Green in Bristol. As a condition of him getting a brown envelope stuffed with beer tokens I asked him to describe his football and real ale experiences and elaborate on his recommendations for best pubs. The description that follows will no doubt strike a chord with those of us who have similar histories of life in the lower leagues, with glories to be remembered for a life time.

My dad first took me to a game circa 1958/59 The sixties were relatively kind to CUFC, particularly at 'Fortress Brunton' and laid the foundation for our promotion to the old First division, those halcyon days when, oh so briefly, we topped the footballing world. Since then the club has indeed embarked on a rollercoaster ride to rival Alton Towers' Corkscrew. Surviving the Knighton days (ball-juggling chairmen, aliens et al), rescued by clubs going bust (before the days of administration and CVA's), a last gasp goal from an on loan keeper, two trips to Wembley, two to Cardiff and a season on loan to non-league oblivion, Actually the season in the conference was reasonably enjoyable but only because we escaped at the first time of asking. Add to that the Supporters' Trust taking the owner to the High Court, and is it any wonder BBC 5Live voted Carlisle the most exciting football club to follow over the last decade.

Last season after a few early setbacks it became very easy to follow Carlisle home and away. Most home games find me in the Rugby Club where they serve 2 regular beers, Yates and Theakston, and a guest. Amongst the away trips last year I particularly enjoyed our trip to The Crown in Stockport, most impressed by the 14 hand pumps and especially the fact that none of them was serving Robinson's despite the pressure from the brewery barons on the local council. Dave and I took our preparation seriously when we visited Bristol and arranged to meet up with Stedders in The Inn on the Green before our visit to the Memorial Ground. The Cemetery in Rochdale should be included on the itinerary for all visiting fans, well worth the extra couple of minutes walk from the ground. We were lucky when visiting Mansfield that it coincided with St George's weekend celebrations and a beer festival at The Bold Forester where the landlord not only took a pride in his beers but seemed pleased to share his enthusiasm with fellow topers. Another favourite, as recommended for inclusion in the guide was the Railway View in Macclesfield, only 10 minutes from the ground, 'beers well kept and good craic.'

The results of the competition are published on the website. There will be another one next year and anyone can win. I hope Mally enjoys the beers he might well buy his mates over the year. It is just a shame that our teams are parting company. If you visit the Carlisle Rugby club please say hello to him for me, I know you will have a good time in what is the best place to drink before a game when visiting Brunton Park.

Mally and his mates, in the Kings Head, Carlisle, celebrating his win as England thrash Sweden (not)

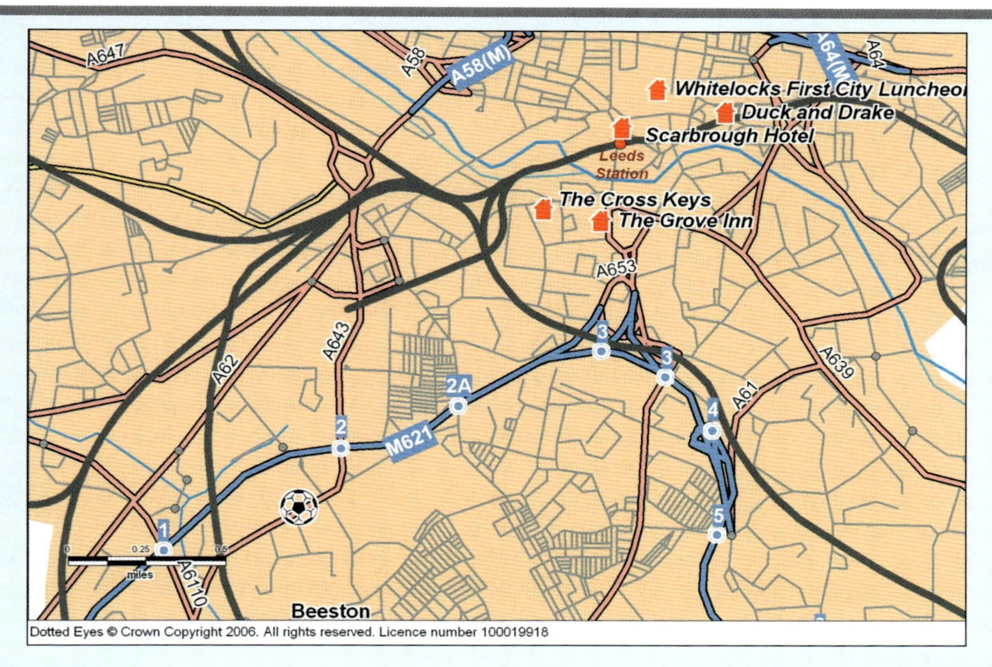

The Cross Keys

107 Water Lane, The Round Foundry, LS11 5WD. Telephone 01132 433711
Gaffer: Cat Thom
Food: Modern British gastro pub fayre with the finest locally sourced seasonal ingredients 12 to 4, 6 to 10. 12 to 6 special menu Sun
Separate smoking areas
Open: 12 to 11 Mon to Sat, 12 to 10.30 Sun

New

MP BM D

As city centres are redeveloped there is usually a trend whereby the old pubs are demolished and replaced with glass fronted warehouse bistros. The Round Foundry is an area of Holgate undergoing such a transformation and the Cross Keys is a remarkable example of how pub destruction need not happen. This pub has not been open for 70 years. The décor is simple, consisting of exposed wooden beams, and brick walls, plain paint but not in trendy pastels. The ales are from an ever -changing beer selection, ideal for real ale enthusiasts.

It trades to the local office workers as a gastro-pub. This food also passed my own student appreciation test when I revisited on a typically busy Friday lunch time. The feel is very continental; this will become more evident during the summer months when the pub spills out into the enclosed quadrangle. While chatting to Jenny it was evident that they are very proud of the spotless, warm and cosy nature of this brand new pub. The competition to real ale is more likely to come from the wine list than the lager selection, although it includes some impressive world ales. Those who were doing so sat in the refectory style bar area, while I joined the ale drinking regulars near the open fire. This pub was recommended by those at the Grove, cheers Shane a good choice.

BWV 28.2.06: Cottage ***Great Western***, Mordue ***Radgie Gadget***, Rooster's ***Black Habit***, ***Yankee***

Duck and Drake

43 Kirkgate, LS2 7DR. Telephone 01132 459728
www.duckanddrake.com
Gaffer: Tracy Valentine
Food: Famous sandwiches, Mon to Sat
Smoking Throughout
Open: 11 to 11 Sun to Wed, 11 to 12 Thu to Sat

Both bars in this nationally known boozer have a similar straightforward, drinking-house style. It is the ale and the atmosphere that sells the pub, alongside great humour, quality ale selection and space to stand and chat. It makes this a perfect place for a group of real ale tickers to meet. It is a venue for serious music, earnest beer sampling and serious conversation. I enjoyed just listening to the craic and gazing at the railway viaduct through the window. The best time to see the pub in its glory is on one of the noisier evening sessions when live music is being played or when the clubbers are mixing with the serious real ale pub crawlers. The atmosphere can positively jump.
UPDATE: Check their website for dates of April Beer Festival.

BWV 13.5.05: Big Lamp ***Bitter***, Caledonian ***80/-***, Elgood's ***Cambridge***, Fuller's ***London Pride***, John Smith's Cask Bitter, Outlaw ***Silver Lining***, Timothy Taylor ***Landlord***, Theakston's ***Best***, ***Mild***, ***Old Peculier***, Wickwar ***IKB***, Weston's ***Old Rosie***
BWV 28.2.06: Caledonian ***Deuchars IPA***, Clark's ***Golden Hornet***, Fuller's ***London Pride***, Goose Eye ***No Eye Deer***, John Smith's ***Cask Bitter***, Mordue ***Five Bridge Bitter***, Timothy Taylor ***Landlord***, Theakston's ***Old Peculier***, Village ***Old Raby Ale***, York ***Bitter***, Weston's ***Old Rosie***

The Grove Inn

Back Row, off Victoria Street, Holbeck, LS11 5PL. Telephone 01132 439254
Gaffer: Rachel Scordos
Food: Cheap and cheerful sandwiches and chips menu 12 to 2 Mon to Fri, 1 to 3 Sun, Not Sat
Separate smoking areas
Open: 12 to 11 Mon to Sat, 12 to 10.30 Sun

The Grove is the home of Doughnut of Guardian pub review fame, top hot blues, arts and craft groups, folk clubs, dancers, singers, rock bands and pardon me, I nearly forgot, top quality real ale.

As the picture shows the Grove is remarkable if only because it is still here, as all around is redeveloped at a sky-high level. John has been here for 16 years and probably seen all there is to see in a great local. The pub is from the beautiful eccentric mold, a corridor pub that has been extended but features beautiful tiny snugs that must play a part in maintaining its future. It was actually a conversion of cottages c1830 with an inter war extension that created the room that hosts the bands. Those bands are legendary and include some world famous names that are reputed to drop in on the Wednesday jamming sessions. One such famous guitarist was turned down by the Hot Pot Belly band, but it didn't affect his career long term. Some of you will know of Brenda Croker and Dave Phillips who regularly appear here. The pub is not however, a music dive. It is a proper pub in every sense of the term and, being handy for the buses to Elland Road, is good for a great lunch time pint or two.

BWV 28.2.06: Adnams ***Broadside***, Caledonian ***80/-***, ***Deuchars IPA***, Daleside ***Bitter***, Dent ***Aviator***, E&S ***Elland Beyond the Pale***, Fernandes ***Pride of Wakefield***, Moorhouses ***Black Cat***, Wells ***Bombardier***

Scarborough Hotel

New

Bishopsgate Street, LS1 5DY. Telephone 01132 434590
Gaffer: Toby Flint
Food: Classic pub menu 11 to 9
Separate smoking areas
Open: 11 to 12, 12 to 10.30 Sun

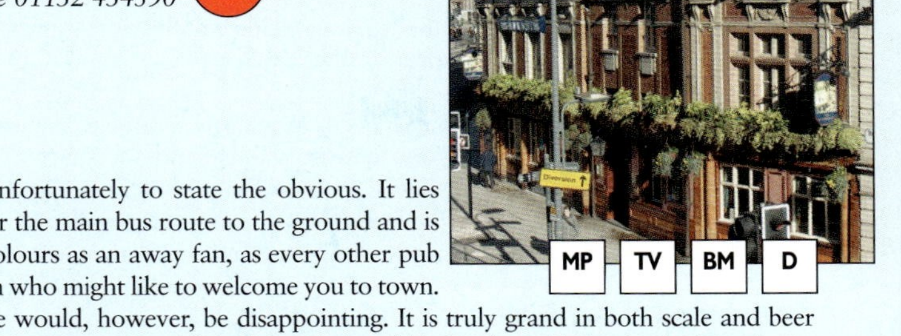

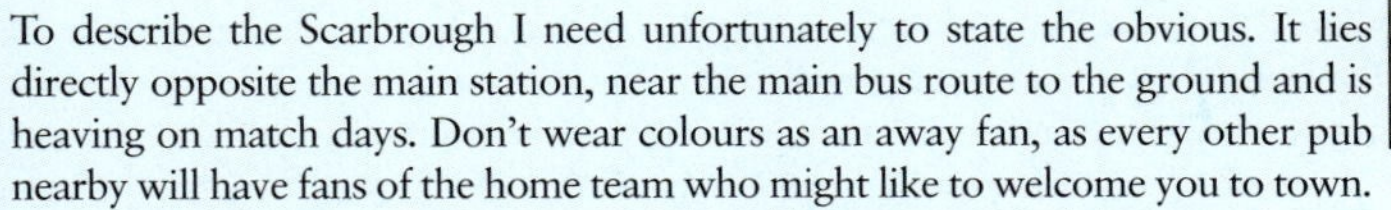

To describe the Scarbrough I need unfortunately to state the obvious. It lies directly opposite the main station, near the main bus route to the ground and is heaving on match days. Don't wear colours as an away fan, as every other pub nearby will have fans of the home team who might like to welcome you to town.

To miss the Scarbrough experience would, however, be disappointing. It is truly grand in both scale and beer choice. It is the local CAMRA pub of the year and is the perfect starting point for the real ale crawl of Leeds city centre. Tetley's are permanent and up to fifteen different beers will be sampled if one was to visit every day of the week. Those who do this include students and office workers. The pub asks '*Are you worthy*?' Of course we are, we can appreciate the beer and friendly atmosphere. I would make this my local for a long weekend visit. It would be great for this to coincide with one of their regular beer festivals. The last one specialised on the theme of Yorkshire day and included ales and cheeses from the county. The locals say they can get to their seats in the ground in 15 minutes. Make it 2.15 to be sure, catching the bus from the aptly named '*dark bridge*' bus stops opposite

BWV 28.2.06: Castle Rock ***Curlew***, Goose Eye ***Pommie's Revenge***, Ossett ***Black Bull***, ***Snowdrop***, Tetley's ***Cask Bitter***, ***Imperial***, Wylam ***Gold Tankard***, Burrow Hill ***Country Cider***, Weston's ***Old Rosie***, ***Perry***

Whitelocks First City Luncheon Bar

Turks Head Yard, LS1 6HB. Telephone 01132 453950
Gaffer: Dave Schol
Food: Home made good value and quality menu 12 to 7, 12 to 5 Sun
Separate smoking areas
Open: 11 to 11, 12 to 10.30 Sun

mirror clad, the pub highly polished and the bar decoratively tiled. The pub still looks tiny, cosy and absolutely fantastic. Nowhere is more than a few paces from the bar, there is no music and the place hums to the sound of small groups in earnest conversation. It soon fills up and spills over into the narrow alley that connects to the real world of busy shoppers parading along the streets nearby. The place fills up with couples, groups of students and early evening beer hunters. It was the obvious pub to take my student niece out to lunch. It is something to cherish, even down to the sobriety testing climb to the toilets.
UPDATE: Dave has taken over and improvements planned include opening the '*top bar*', i.e. extending further along the alleyway.

BWV 13.3.05: Daleside ***Stout***, John Smith's ***Cask Bitter***, Theakston's ***Old Peculier***, Wells ***John Bull***, ***Bombardier***, York Brewery ***Cascade***
BWV 28.2.06: Caledonian ***Deuchars IPA***, Durham ***Definitive***, Itchen Valley ***Pure Gold***, John Smith's ***Cask Bitter***, Mordue ***Geordie Pride***, Theakston's ***Best***, ***Old Peculier***, Wentworth ***Challenge***

Leeds

Leeds is a city that sprawls. From the fly blown outer reaches to the spread out centre it is a place easy to get lost in. It is also the only British city with a population big enough to support two professional football clubs, but which has only ever had one.

The worst thing about the layout of Leeds for visitors was the large distance between the train and bus station, but things have been improved beyond measure with the introduction of a bus linking the two. It is free, at present, and because of the one way system it takes you on a tour of the centre, including some of older Georgian parts. Be warned though, once you get to the bus station you are likely to discover that the bus you need does not come anywhere near it, and has to be hunted out like a Roman lavatory in a Time Team telly program.

Museum and Art Gallery

These are next to the Town Hall. The gallery has a good collection of Atkinson Grimshaw paintings. He was born in Leeds and was a driving force for the opening of this gallery in 1888. His paintings of night time, rain soaked cities are redolent of life in a northern town in a way that matchstick men never could be. There is also a Henry Moore gallery. He spent his whole life telling everybody about his importance to art, and quite a few took him at his own valuation.

Leicester

A rich, big, and ancient town, with one of the few Roman walls in England taller than a metre. It was an important textile town, but never really suffered the boom and bust lifestyle some northern towns endured, but neither does it have grand monuments to industrial profits and personal vanity. You could spend an excellent day here though, and it has one of Britain's highest per capita concentrations of museums: but for all that it somehow lacks spark. You can draw your own conclusions from the fact that Leicester is most famous for Walkers crisps and Gary Lineker. The two probably fill the folk of Leicester, and Lineker's accountant, with a warm glow.

The National Gas Museum

A cultural highlight. There is something about gas that appeals to the depths of man. Woman however may take a different view. Bradwan hopes this place will solve a philosophical question that has been troubling us for years while we sit in the pub with our mouths open. Why don't gas holders leak? They go up and down but no gas escapes.
www.gasmuseum.co.uk

Leicester Council runs nine museums and an art gallery. We suggest:

The Jewry Wall Museum

This is a good historical museum based near the Roman wall we mentioned.

The Abbey Pumping Station

A fine museum, built around four magnificent beam engines that spent their lives pumping Leicester's sewage. They also have a coal fired chip van and a 'famous' interactive loo.
www.leicestermuseums.ac.uk/museums

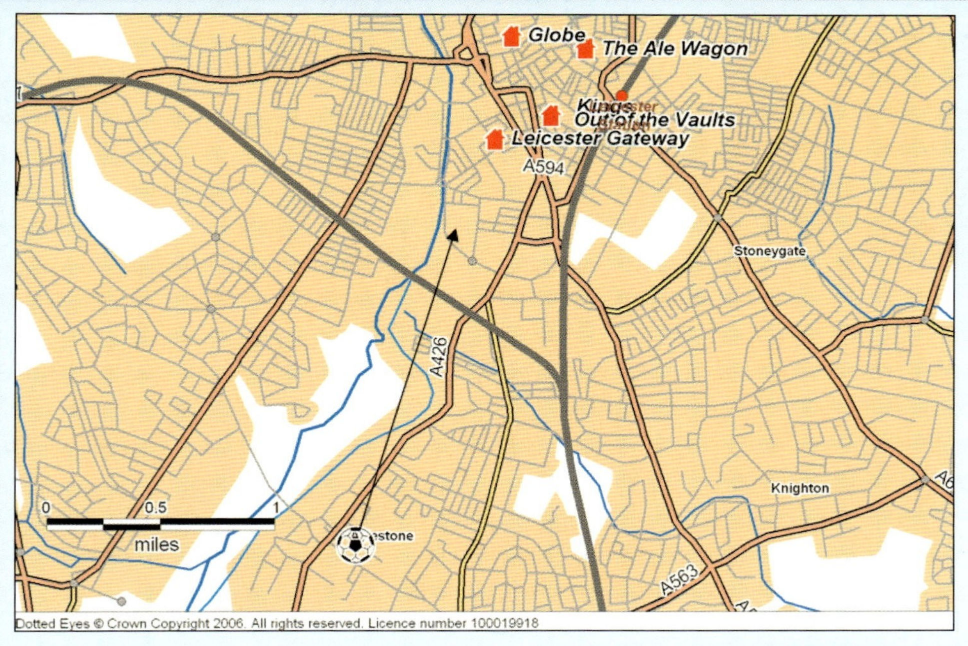

The Ale Wagon

27 Rutland Street, LE1 1RE. Telephone 01162 623330
Gaffers: Stephen Hoskins and family
Food: Traditional pub menu TBA
Smoking Throughout
Open: 11 to 11, 12 to 3, 7 to 10.30 Sun

MP BM D

The concept of a family run pub is stretched to fantastic lengths at the Ale Wagon. Steve owns the pub, Phil is the cellar man and Daphne, their sister, is doubtless the organising brains behind the brothers' brawn. Hoskins Brothers brews are new to me and the Ale Wagon is a keen recommendation for the style and atmosphere to be found in this great street corner town pub. The beers are brewed at present by Tower brewery. There are plans to brew on the site and when that happens no doubt the pub will become even more popular.

The Ale Wagon has two separate bars. The first room is to the right, decked with photos and without a view of the full beer range. I, along with the regulars, preferred the longer left hand bar that is impressive in its simplicity. The samples are provided and the beer described by knowledgeable staff, then you can be left to enjoy the ale without distraction, or as in my case, join in a discussion with the locals who were willing to engage this weary traveller. The clientele include the usual local office workers but also many of Leicester's more artistic and literary folk. The comedy nights attracted my eye. I was amused to earwig on a booking by the local TUC; beer and sandwiches are very appropriate here. All this and regular beer festivals, make this a pub I will revisit when the opportunity next arises.

BWV 5.4.06: Archers ***Spring Blonde***, Hoskins Brothers ***EXS***, ***Gaggle and Titter***, ***HOB***, ***HOB Best Mild***, ***Little Matty***, ***Tom Kelly's Stout***, ***White Dolphin Wheat Beer***, Tower ***Bitter***

Globe

43 Silver Street, LE1 5EU. Telephone 01162 629819
Gaffer: Hugh Kerr
Food: Good value traditional meals 12 to 7
Smoking Throughout
Open: 11 to 11, 12 to 10.30 Sun

The Globe has a central bar and several drinking rooms of differing size, thus making this town boozer a welcome relief from the city centre bustle. This could be in a village, or in the biggest city. It has the essential design features to make it both intimate and a great meeting place. The wooden floors and simple furniture made this user concentrate on the beer and good conversation. *'The Globe is an oasis of calm in the city streets well known for their theme bars.'* The food was typical accompaniment to good real ale, simple and hearty. The conversation in early afternoon was also of the type often found in a central pub frequented by professionals and local residents alike. While the crowds head for nearby boys pubs I would always find myself gravitating to the Globe, it offers so much more to me in terms of real pub atmosphere and service with a smile.
UPDATE: Nothing much has changed. This year I visited this pub in a more sober state and found more hidden gems. Sunchaser is now a regular beer in the list.

BWV 15.11.04: Everards ***Beacon***, ***Equinox***, ***Original***, ***Tiger***.
BWV 5.4.06 Courage ***Directors***, Everards ***All Black***, ***Beacon***, ***Buddings***, ***Original***, ***Sunchaser***, ***Tiger***

Kings

30 King Street, LE1 6RL. Telephone 0777 394172 **New**
Gaffer: Shanti Odedra
Food: Reasonably priced good quality traditional menu 12 to 2. No food Sun
Smoking Throughout
Open: 11 to 11, 12 to 10.30 Sun

When reading my guide it became evident to me that the large influence of the Tigers on real ale pubs in town. Therefore my hunt this year wanted to find a genuine real ale pub that offers essential football factors found in most other cities. The Kings offers this and more. The ales are always rotating from a national selection with no regular ale. The TVs are supplemented by a large pull down screen and the greeting at all times is both friendly and welcoming.

The pub is basically one long room, separated into two areas by a set of steps and extended beyond in summer when the courtyard traps the sun. The football attractions continue with the sight of football shirts hanging from the ceiling and in the evenings when City players are known to use this as their local in town. Don't be fooled into thinking it is youngsters bar. It is a great pub in its normal mode. It is a place where couples meet up for a date over lunch, where business meetings are clinched and where friends meet pre and post shopping. The enthusiasm for real ale among the young staff is infectious and no doubt the reputation will be made in time through the quality of the ale rather than any football connections. Shanti, Carl and James make a great team and the Kings has certainly proven to be a satisfying find.

BWV 5.4.06: Caledonian ***Deuchars IPA***, Fuller's ***London Pride***, Shepherd Neame ***Spitfire***

Leicester Gateway

52 Gateway Street, LE2 7DP. Telephone 01162 557319
Gaffer: Peter McWilliam
Food: Good quality menu based on locally sourced produce all day
Smoking Throughout
Open: 11 to 11 Mon to Fri, 12 to 10.30 Sun Open at 11 on match days

F

MP SKY BM D

In student and nurses' land, this pub caters for those who need quick service before moving on. As a result the bar is large and has plenty of standing room and has menus that change with the clientele. Families of Tigers and Foxes create a friendly atmosphere. Saturday lunchtime often sees away fans who know that City fans will be '*bringing sons and daughters to a good, spacious pub that serves good food and real ale*.' During the day I visited there was a distinct lunchtime student trade. The locals suggest that the Gateway has become famous as a real ale meeting place. This is a place to set the tone for an evening beer strolling around the town. The quality of the ale selection is certainly something to get you in the mood for Leicestershire's finest. A good riverside walk to the ground makes it good for the pre match pint in town.
UPDATE: Tiger and XXXB are regular weekend ales. Themed brewery nights are a new feature; check the website for further details.

BWV 15.11.04: Abbeydale ***Absolution***
BWV 5.4.06: Castle Rock ***Elsie Mo***, ***Harvest Pale***, ***Hemlock***, Nelson ***England Expects***

Out of the Vaults

24 King Street, LE1 6R. Telephone 07976 222378
Gaffer: Paul Summers
Food: Awesome filled baguettes all day
Smoking Throughout
Open: 12 to 11, 12 to 10.30 Sun

The much loved Vaults has gone but Paul continues the tradition with a pub devoted to his love of small micro-breweries. The bar is long and narrow with entrances on both sides. '*The beers are always different, never the same two days running*.' Don't forget the range of continental lagers. As Phil Passingham of Market Harborough says '*Locals and away fans can mix and enjoy a whole array of well kept ales from regional and micro brewers*.'
UPDATE: The list of new breweries continues to amaze. The pub will open earlier for big games. The pub now sponsors a local football team. Beer festivals are now well established on the local real ale scene, being held every other month.

BWV 15.11.04 Abbeydale ***Matins***, ***Devotion***, Beowulf ***Finns Hall Porter***, Facers ***Landslide***, Glentworth ***Happy Hooker***, Goose Eye ***Pommies Revenge***, Oakham ***Bishops Farewell***, ***White Dwarf***, Upper Agbrigg ***Autumn Special***, Woodlands ***Midnight Stout***, Biddenham ***Bushels Cider***, Weston's ***Old Rosie***
BWV 5.4.06: Atomic ***Reactor***, Fun Fair ***Showman's Gold***, Goff's ***Launcelot***, Leatherbritches ***The Oak***, Oakham ***Bishops Fare***well, ***Harlequin Ale***, ***White Dwarf***, ***Red Squirrel Irish Stout***, Salamander ***Double Bill,*** Wissey Valley ***Saucy Spice***

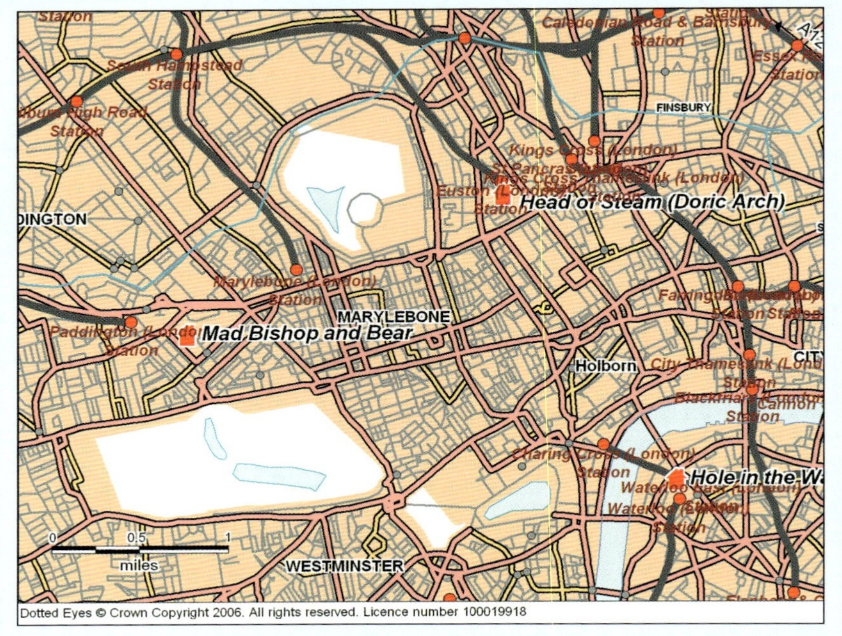

Head of Steam (Doric Arch) Euston Station

1 Eversholt Street, Euston, NW1 1DN. Telephone 020 7383 3359
www.theheadofsteam.co.uk
Gaffer: Dave O'Sullivan
Food: New menu, quality pub food 12 to 2.30, 5 to 9, 12 to 5 Sat
Separate smoking areas
Open: 11 to 11, 12 to 6 Sun

A station pub as they used to be? No, not cold and draughty, but with railway signs, carriage seating, friendly, helpful staff and a feeling that it's OK to miss the train because who wants to rush anyway. The Head of Steam name is spreading but this version still leads the way in creating a real ale club virtually on the station concourse. There are usually up to nine ever-changing real ales. When planning my journeys home it has always been a place to factor in to travel times, i.e. wherever you are leave time for the HoS before getting the train from Euston. It has one large bar that is creatively split into separate areas and levels. The TVs are very discrete I particularly like to find space in what looks like a mini-railway carriage complete with no smoking signs and bench seats so close to each other you can read the paper of your fellow commuter.
UPDATE: Fullers have taken it into their fold but guests continue. A refurbishment of the frontage may include the new name but only plasma screens and furnishings will add a touch of modernism.

BWV 6.12.04: Banks's ***Original***, Black Sheep ***Bitter***, Caledonian ***Santa's Little Helper***, Dark Star ***Porter***, ***Special Edition***, Weston's ***Vintage Cider***
BWV 1.11.05: Archers ***Village***, Cottage ***Western Glory***, Fuller's ***Discovery***, ***ESB***, London ***Pride***, ***Trafalgar***, Hopback ***GFB***, Phoenix ***White Tornado***, Weston's ***Old Rosie***, ***Vintage Ciders***

Hole in the Wall

New

5 Mepham Street, Waterloo, SE1 8SQ. Telephone 020 7928 6196
Gaffer: Chris Elliott
Food: Good traditional food cooked to order 12 to 7.30, 12 to 4 Sun
Smoking Throughout
Open: 11 to 11, 12 to 10.30 Sun

The Hole in the Wall is a pub underneath the Arches immediately outside the main entrance to Waterloo Station. It has, therefore, some very unusual design features and a character that is like few others in Britain. There are two rooms, one small and snug the other large and canteen like, both with the rumble of overhead railways to agitate the beer.

This Freehouse has been in the same family for a very long time. In its present form it is well known for offering rarer ales, on my visit it was the Battersea ale that drew my eye. Whenever I have gone in it has been very busy. The people are fairly transient so it is best to go into the back room where there is space and often a table to sit around and watch sports on the large TV. Ian the Morton fan of a manager was keen to stress that this is a no colours pub and that the locals are very much regular commuters. Many will be Railway workers of the Eurostar type. Andy my train driving mate being one such advocate of the HITW. On Rugby international days the pub will be heaving, so too when away fans are travelling home and wanting a quick pint before the train home. The bar menu will be limited on such days but the beer menu likely to be at its most extensive. It has a heart in the traditions of a proper London Boozer. a good welcome and conversation is guaranteed at any time of the day.

BWV 22.3.06: Adnams ***Best***, ***Broadside***, Battersea ***Bitter***, Fuller's ***London Pride***, Shepherd Neame ***Spitfire***, Young's ***Bitter***, ***Special***

Mad Bishop and Bear

The Lawn, Paddington Station, W2 1HB. Telephone 020 740 22441
Gaffer: David and Chad
Food: Traditional pub-food from pastries to steaks 9 to 9
Separate smoking areas
Open: 9 to 11 Mon to Fri, 7.30 to 11 Sat, 10 to 10.30 Sun

In my opinion this is the best designed London station bar. It takes elements of classic pub design (tiled floors and mirrors, etc.) and integrates them into a large, modern terminus waiting bar, complete with two plasma screens for TV matches. The good, friendly staff and quality ale make this ideal for meeting up and planning your visit to London. Large and comfortable, but retaining the design features that allow for quiet supping, the Mad Bishop and Bear is whatever you want it to be. As a footie fan you might need to dodge the crowds of fellow fans in colours to be allowed through Sushi land to the bar. Alternatively, for London fans going west catch a breakfast and beer before the train journey out west. Sit on the terrace to get the full interest of being in one of GWR's beautiful stations.
UPDATE: Clare has moved on – most be something in the beer! The pub is as busy as ever. I visited half a dozen times over the season and it never disappointed.

BWV 20.12.04: Fuller's ***Chiswick***, ***ESB***, ***London Porter***, ***London Pride***
BWV 1.2.06: Fuller's ***Chiswick***, ***Discovery***, ***ESB***, ***London Pride***

The league tables are given because many of you may only travel to a few games away from home a season. When you do it might involve an overnight stay or a full weekend of beer drinking research and a game. The table should give you the readers choices of which are the best towns and those that might best be left for another year.

The scoring is based on a very crude analysis of:

1 The average number of beers on offer when I visited each pub ABP (Average beer points).

2 A weighted score based on the number of votes each town received when I asked the people to rate their top three towns for football and real ale WVS (Weighted vote score).

3 I then fixed it to get my personal choices at the top.

4 The end result is something that should not be taken too seriously

PREMIERSHIP

	ABP	WVS	TOTAL
NEWCASTLE	4.5	15	19.5
MAN CITY	8	5	13
PORTSMOUTH	5.3	5	10.3
SHEFFIELD U	7	3	10
TOTTENHAM	7.6	2	9.6
MAN UNITED	3.5	5	8.5
ASTON VILLA	7.4	0	7.4
EVERTON	7	0	7
BOLTON	4.2	2	6.2
CHELSEA	4	2	6
WEST HAM	4	2	6
LIVERPOOL	5.6	0	5.6
BLACKBURN	3.4	2	5.4
ARSENAL	3	2	5
READING	4.75	0	4.75
FULHAM	2.66	2	4.66
WATFORD	4.6	0	4.6
CHARLTON	2.33	2	4.33
MIDDLESBORO	2.8	1	3.8
WIGAN	3.6	0	3.6

CHAMPIONSHIP

	ABP	WVS	TOTAL
DERBY	7.1	9	16.1
NORWICH	11.4	2	13.4
SHEFFIELD W	9	4	13
IPSWICH	10.7	1	11.7
BIRMINGHAM	8.7	0	8.7
WEST BROM	3.6	5	8.6
LEEDS	8	0	8
SOUTHAMPTON	6	1	7
BURNLEY	5.5	1	6.5
LEICESTER	6.2	0	6.2
SUNDERLAND	5.7	0	5.7
COVENTRY	5.6	0	5.6
WOLVES	5.5	0	5.5
STOKE	5.4	0	5.4
PRESTON	5	0	5
CARDIFF	5	0	5
HULL	4.9	0	4.9
LUTON	4.8	0	4.8
SOUTHEND	4.5	0	4.5
PLYMOUTH	4.5	0	4.5
BARNSLEY	4.2	0	4.2
COLCHESTER	4	0	4
QPR	3.33	0	3.33
CRYSTAL PALACE	2.66	0	2.66

DIVISION ONE

	ABP	WVS	TOTAL
NOTTINGHAM F	9.1	6	15.1
BRADFORD	8.7	2	10.7
HUDDERSFIELD	7.8	2	9.8
CHESTERFIELD	8.1	0	8.1
BLACKPOOL	5	3	8
LEYTON ORIENT	5	2	7
BRISTOL C	5.2	1	6.2
BRIGHTON	6	0	6
MILLWALL	3.66	2	5.66
NORTHAMPTON	5.1	0	5.1
TRANMERE	5.1	0	5.1
ROTHERHAM	5	0	5
DONCASTER	4.8	0	4.8
PORT VALE	4.7	0	4.7
SWANSEA	4.6	0	4.6
BOURNEMOUTH	4.6	0	4.6
CREWE	4.6	0	4.6
CHELTENHAM	4.4	0	4.4
GILLINGHAM	4.1	0	4.1
SCUNTHORPE	4	0	4
BRENTFORD	4	0	4
OLDHAM	3.4	0	3.4
YEOVIL	3	0	3
CARLISLE	2.6	0	2.6

DIVISION TWO

	ABP	WVS	TOTAL
PETERBOROUGH	9.4	8	17.4
LINCOLN	6	8	14
NOTTS CO	7.5	6	13.5
SHREWSBURY	6.4	7	13.4
DARLINGTON	6.8	4	10.8
STOCKPORT	8.6	1	9.6
CHESTER	4.6	4	8.6
WALSALL	6.8	0	6.8
HEREFORD	6.6	0	6.6
BRISTOL R	5.5	1	6.5
MANSFIELD	6	0	6
BURY	5.6	0	5.6
ROCHDALE	4.3	1	5.3
SWINDON	5.25	0	5.25
GRIMSBY	5	0	5
MACCLESFIELD	3.8	1	4.8
BOSTON	4	0	4
TORQUAY	3.8	0	3.8
MILTON KEYNES	3.75	0	3.75
WYCOMBE	3.5	0	3.5
ACCRINGTON	3.3	0	3.3
BARNET	3	0	3
HARTLEPOOL	2.5	0	2.5
WREXHAM	2	0	2

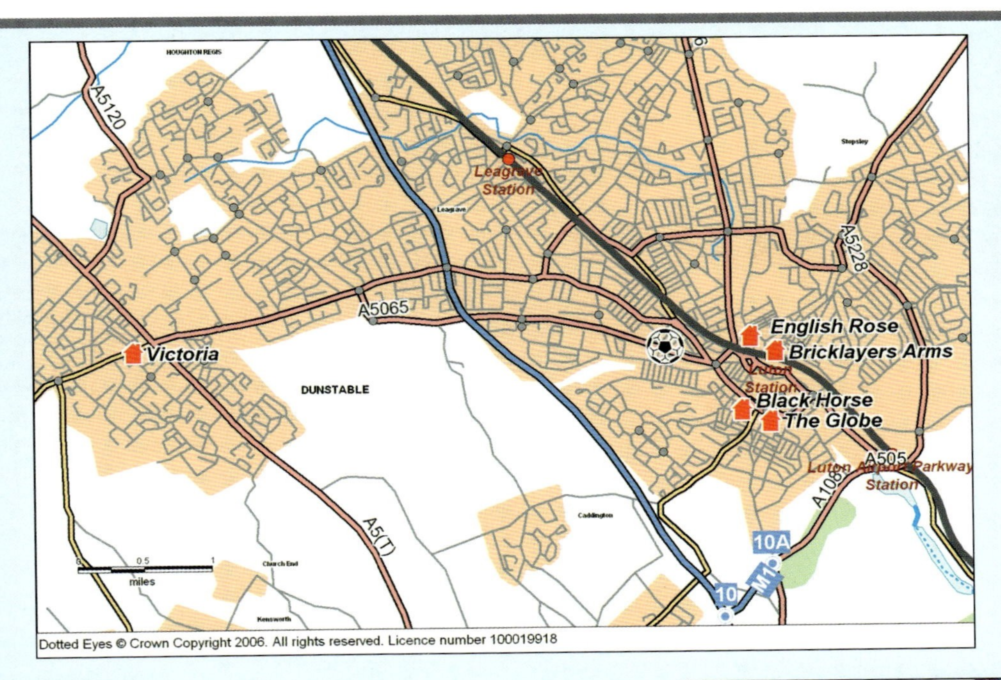

Black Horse

23 Hastings Street, LU1 6BE. Telephone 01582 450994
Gaffer: Jay Massey
Smoking Throughout
Open: 2 to 11 Mon to Fri, 1 to 11 Sat, 1 to 10.30 Sun

B

SP | TV | JB | PG | D

John bought the pub in May 2005 and it soon became established as a valuable addition to the Luton real ale circuit. The pub offers a wide range of micro brews and independent ales with a frequency that says that *'if you blink you will miss it.'*

The pub is another of the back-street locals that make up the best that Luton has to offer. This is the nearest to the ground and just around the corner from the now closed Two Brewers. It will be busy on a matchday with the real ale drinking Hatters who find it a convenient stopping off point on the way uphill to the ground. The number of pump clips covering the cream and red walls was increasing so fast that by the time you visit next season there might well be no wall space to find. The pub also has real fires and a great patio area to entice the non regulars to visit in both summer and winter. The pub held a beer festival in November and another was planeed for April.

UPDATE: The excellent local CAMRA guide *'Beer in Beds'* reported in May that *'The pub is now run by Steph and Kirsty who regulars know as they have worked there for some time as bar staff. Many recent visits have found no change in the beer range or quality.'*

BWV 15.12.05: Archers ***Archers Arrow***, ***Blindmans Eclipse***, Oakham ***White Dwarf***, Tring ***Side Pocket***, ***Wicked Wiggy***

Bricklayers Arms

14-16 High Town Road, LU2 0DD. Telephone 01582 611017
Gaffer: Alison Taylor
Food: Good value pub menu 12 to 2 Mon to Fri, Rolls on Sun
Smoking Throughout
Open: 12 to 3, 5 to 11 Mon to Thu, 12 to 12 Fri and Sat, 12 to 10.30 Sun

On opening time entry this tardis like pub has the feel of a library but soon you see it filling up and it becomes a buzzing junior common room for Hatters and away fans alike. Just out of the back entrance to the station this pub is always busy and always friendly. It has a legendary status among away fans that enjoy '*its proximity to the station but also it being out of the Town centre chain pub circuit.*' Most talk of finding space around the wooden casks and reminiscing of the '*days when High Town had a full run of real ale pubs.*' The highest recommendations come for the staff '*who are very football fan friendly and know that footie and real ale makes for good atmosphere.*' Most important is the welcome you get from Alison; all are like long lost friends. It has been known for footie fans to seek refuge from summer rain while watching local county cricket to appear at the pub and be recognised as footie fans and given a similarly cheery '*Hello, haven't seen you for a while.*' This is definitely a taxi from the pub experience.
UPDATE: The pub is essentially the same with big screens for the world cup.

BWV 22.10.04: B&T ***Golden Hatter***, Everards ***Beacon***, ***Tiger***
BWV 27.6.05: Everards ***Beacon***, ***Tiger***, Nethergate ***Augustinian***, ***Old Chap***, White Horse ***Flibbertigibbet***

English Rose

New

46 Old Bedford Road, LU2 7PA. Telephone 01582 723889
www.englishroseluton.co.uk
Gaffers: Stan and Lisa Smith
Food: Good value traditional pub food 12 to 2 Tue to Fri, 12 to 6 Sat
Smoking Throughout MP TV JB P
Open: 12 to 11

The English Rose is the classic pub that is found just outside almost every town centre in the country. There is however some great differences that make the pub a cut above the rest.

The pub is the local 2006 CAMRA Pub of the year. It has four ales, three of which are ever-changing. The selection often finds beers from every part of the country, often from smaller independent brewers. They describe themselves as '*The village pub in the town*'. By this they mean that the pub has a good regulars feel, they know each other and welcome new visitors into their cherished community. I was once one such newcomer. This was one of my ex colleagues' haunts. The local area has its fair share of young teachers and nurses living in this typical inner city community. The pub is not a sporty pub as such, but it certainly is one for friendly banter and regular good honest fun. The single bar has a pool table. The bar section is standing only, on wooden floors with the occasional stool. The best feature of this pub for footie fans is that there is a great pub garden if it gets very busy. It was recommended by Brentford fans who found it last year. This was a rare event for the pub; it lies off the obvious routes to the ground. It is however, a great choice if you want to see Luton pub life at its friendliest. For me it was off to catch up with some old mates, if they ever answer their phone!

BWV 27.5.06: Brakspear *Bitter*, Elgood's *Black Dog Mild*, Old Mill *Old Curiosity*, York *Decade*

The Globe

26 Union Street, LU1 3AN. Telephone 01582 728681
Gaffers: Ian Mackay and Pat Fallon
Food: Good value traditional pub food 11 to 3 Mon to Sat
Smoking Throughout
Open: 11 to 11

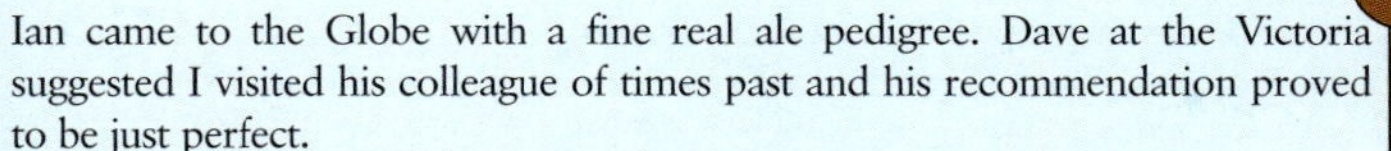

Ian came to the Globe with a fine real ale pedigree. Dave at the Victoria suggested I visited his colleague of times past and his recommendation proved to be just perfect.

The pub is a street corner boozer that lies just south of the town centre inner ring road. It is small and very comfortable; being spotless and sparkling, having a warm glow that in part is due to the Sauna style wooden floors and walls. The beer had a great mix of national ale well served plus new ale for me to tick, if I did tick that is. The pub really is a local community pub. The pub notice board tells of successes in dominoes, quizzes and local Sunday league football. The locals are definitely of the gentle thirty-plus type. They have a mix that reflects the local area, one that finds young professionals as welcome as visiting builders and community workers coming from the nearby council offices. The number of beers has increased to three since Ian arrived. It has a good reputation among the local CAMRA crew. It also has a large patio area that s great for those summer days when a barbecue fits the social bill. If you like to find friendly back - street pubs then this will suit you fine. It is the sort of pub that welcomes you in as a new friend; it will not take long for a new resident to be playing pub games with new found fans of real ale.

BWV 27.5.06: Caledonian ***Deuchars IPA***, Cottage ***Somerset and Dorset***, Greene King ***IPA***

Victoria

69 West Street, Dunstable, LU6 1ST. Telephone 01582 662682
Gaffers: Val and Dave Hobbs
Food: Meals prepared to order (Up to 25 mins.) plus sandwiches and rolls.
12 to 3 Mon to Fri, 12 to 4 Sat, 1 to 4 Sun
Separate smoking areas
Open: 11 to 11 Mon to Sat, 12 to 10.30 Sun

When I am asked what makes a good community pub then the Victoria will instantly come to mind. As Steve of Luton says; '*this is the major real ale pub in Dunstable.*' Val and Dave use every bit of it to pander to real ale lovers. Four constantly changing ales, often from far flung fields, means that there is often a sense of surprise on the menu. It has a heated courtyard garden and back room that four times a year hosts a real ale festival. Most impressive is the board advertising the events of the week that means that sports lovers run, cycle, crawl, climb and kick either to, or for the pub. Who could blame them, this pub is tiny heaven, with humour among the medals on show and sadness in the Arsenal shirt on the wall. The non-league version of this guide would have much to say on just how good this place is, as it is a Dunstable Town fans haunt. David Read sums it up as '*just a great pub.*'
UPDATE: Beer festivals are held on the last weekend of Jan, April, July and October. The pub has upgraded plasma TV screens.

BWV 22.1.04: Freeminer ***Fusion***, Hampshire ***King Alfred's Ale***, Mauldons ***Old Trip***, Ridley's ***Rumpus***, Tring ***Victoria Ale***
BWV 27.6.05: Mighty Oak ***Hornpipe***, Springhead ***Charlie's Angel***, ***St. Peter's Mild***, Tring ***Victoria Ale***

Luton

The Kenilworth Road Stadium is probably the most astonishing thing in Luton. It will never win awards for architecture, but it is not beauty that makes it unique: neither is it because it is one of the very few grounds left that has houses up to the walls; or has one stand made up of conservatories while the others have some truly bizarre angles. No, it is because it is the only ground where some fans have to get in through a terrace of houses. Away fans pay at turnstiles in the front wall of two houses and climb up thin iron stairs that offer fine views of the neighbouring bedrooms, and even bathrooms if they have left the window open!

Luton is a big place, and there is a lot of rebuilding going on, but parts, especially around the station, felt like a little northern town abandoned by industry and hope. We know people who claim it has a 'nice' centre that perhaps lacks interest. The people who know it and do not like it hate it with a passion.

Both of Luton's museums are over a mile out of town, and it really needs some attraction to draw the slack jawed to the centre. If it creates one it would need to improve its layout. We know of no town that so badly combines the English disdain for putting up useful signs, with street planning that offers no clue to which road will take you somewhere, or even anywhere.

Norwich

This city is a cultural highlight.

'Norwich has flourished as the big city in the minds of men for generations. It is no jumped-up conglomeration of factories warehouses and dormitories.'
J.B. Priestley, English Journey

Castle Museum and Art Gallery

The castle is stuck on a hill, not a common thing in Norfolk. We are not going to give directions because if you can't see it you are probably a referees assistant. There are some fine things inside, including water colours of the flat lands and over powering sky of East Anglia by John Sell Cotman and others of the Norwich School.

According to their website there is also a… '***Teapot Gallery***, which contains the greatest specialist collection of British ceramic teapots in the world.' We wonder which museum has the greatest non specialist collection of British ceramic teapots. Does the person in charge of Norwich's teapots spend the waking hours devising cunning plots to undermine the enemy museum and its 'common' British teapot collection? If they are Norfolk bred we doubt it. It is an area famous for solid fighters, not subtle schemers. Oliver Cromwell and most of his Ironsides came from East Anglia, and while your chance of survival would have been slim if they were charging towards you singing Psalms, you would not have needed to worry over much about one of them trying to sell you a time-share in a Wexford turf hut, or writing slanderous lies about you in other people's hymn books.
www.norfolk.gov.uk

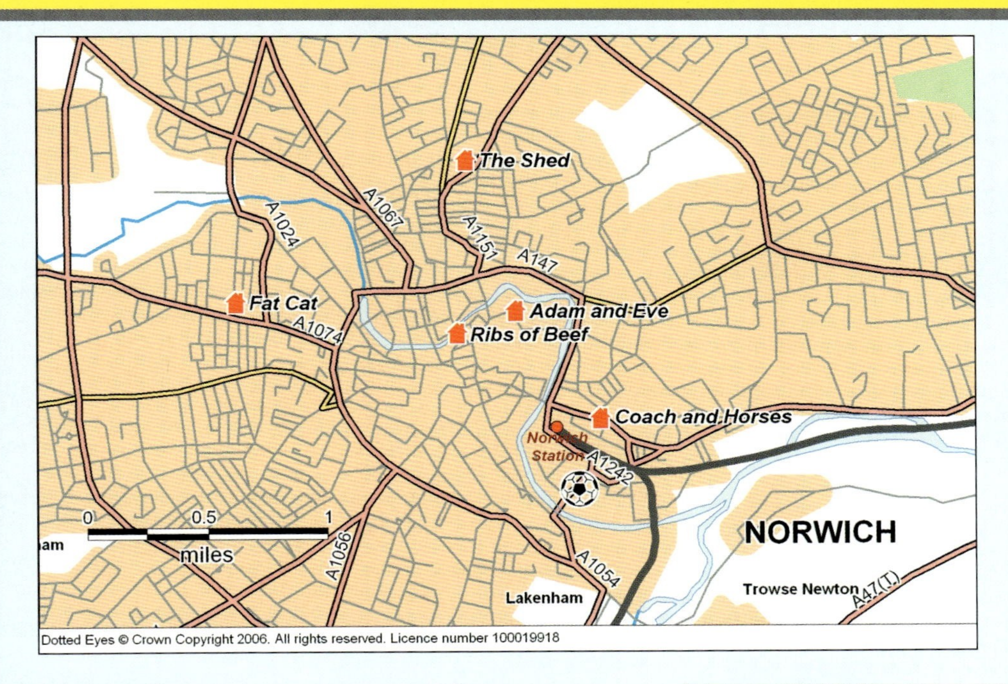

Adam and Eve

New

Bishopgate, NR3 1R2. Telephone 01603 667423
Gaffer Rita McCluskey
Food: Daily specials add to the extensive pie, bakes and fish menu
12 to 7, 12 to 2.30 Sun
Separate smoking areas
Open: 11 to 11, 12 to 10.30 Sun

CP BM

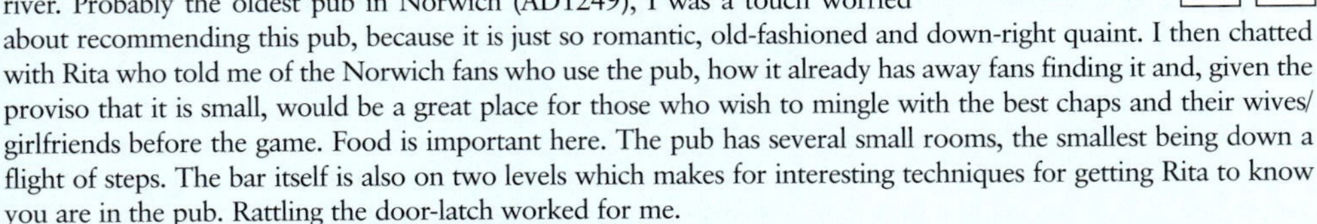

As the picture shows, this really is a country gem in the heart of the cathedral district, and it is also within easy walk of the ground, station, city centre and river. Probably the oldest pub in Norwich (AD1249), I was a touch worried about recommending this pub, because it is just so romantic, old-fashioned and down-right quaint. I then chatted with Rita who told me of the Norwich fans who use the pub, how it already has away fans finding it and, given the proviso that it is small, would be a great place for those who wish to mingle with the best chaps and their wives/girlfriends before the game. Food is important here. The pub has several small rooms, the smallest being down a flight of steps. The bar itself is also on two levels which makes for interesting techniques for getting Rita to know you are in the pub. Rattling the door-latch worked for me.

My visit also coincided with an infamous trial in the nearby courts. It was mildly amusing to write these notes under the suspicious eyes of court witnesses and then even funnier to see their reaction as court officials entered for their lunchtime ale and meal. The cheese and ale soup appeared to be highly recommended. For me it was the Old Peculier that drew my attention as I moved from the toll-gate room into the main bar.

BWV 19.1.06: Adnams ***Bitter***, Greene King ***IPA***, Theakston's ***Old Peculier***, Wells ***Bombardier***

Coach and Horses

82 Thorpe Road, NR1 1BA. Telephone 01603 677077
www.thecoachthorperoad.co.uk

B

Gaffer Bob Cameron
Food: Home-prepared and locally-sourced menu, from rolls to steak and fish specialities 11 to 9, 11 to 8 Sun
Smoking Throughout
Open: 11 to 12, 11 to 1 Fri and Sat

This is a deceptively large pub with a great atmosphere. *'Visitors to Norwich should not miss out on this ale drinker's paradise.'* (CAMRA 2004) The home of the Chalk Hill micro-brewery offers a full range including a mild and a variety of strengths and styles. *'On my visits, it has been absolutely heaving, with plenty from both sides and drinkers spilling onto the outside drinking area, all getting on perfectly well, the way things should be.'* (London Clarets) My visits were very different and equally brilliant. One visit found masses of fans eating and sampling quality ales unavailable in their own town. My second trip it was the locals, particularly posties and office workers, on a regular relaxed lunchtime session. How lucky are Norwich fans to have this fantastic brewery tap so close to the ground?
UPDATE: An outside bar is now operating on matchdays. *'Drinking Consultants'* have set up in the front. It remains truly great.

BWV 21.9.04: Chalk Hill ***Brewery Tap***, ***Dreadnought***, ***Flintknappers Mild***, ***Old Tackle***, ***Winters Golden***, Banham ***Cider***
BWV 19.1.06: Chalk Hill ***Brewery Tap***, ***CHB***, ***Dreadnought***, ***Flintknappers Mild***, ***Gold***, ***Old Tackle***, Theakston's ***Best***, Burnard's ***Cider***

Ribs of Beef

41 Wensum Street, NR3 1HY. Telephone 01603 619517

F

Gaffer Rorie Bradshaw
Food: Wholesome homemade menu with specialities and vegetarian options 12 to 2.30, 12 to 5 at weekends
Separate smoking areas
Open: 11 to 11, 11 to 12 Sat, 12 to 11 Sun

This two-level pub, next to the river in the centre of town, is perfect for the weekend visitor to town. It is busy at lunchtime, catering for a range of people so wide that you begin to wonder whether real ale is having a greater pull on the young here than in the rest of the UK. The extensive list of real ales is constantly changing and has a true East Anglian flavour in the selection. This is a great pub for a good pub-style lunchtime meal, or as an evening meeting place, for as their website says, *'a refreshing pint on the jetty.'* The lower level bar has direct access to the river-front. It also has TV screens that are positioned so well that it is possible to watch games from any seat in this excellent pub. While there are many good pubs in town the location of the Ribs is something special.
UPDATE: New chef Alison is in the process of further improving the menu. The pub is still great.

BWV 1.2.05: Adnams ***Bitter***, Burton Bridge ***Damson Porter***, Courage ***Best***, Elgood's ***Black Dog Mild***, Mauldons ***White Adder***, St. Peter's ***Lemon and Ginger***, Wentworth ***WPA***, Caledonian ***80/-***, Norfolk ***Medium Dry Cider***
BWV 19.1.06: Adnams ***Bitter***, ***Old Ale***, ***Tally-ho***! Courage ***Best***, Newby Wyke ***Black Squall***, Oulton ***Mudford Mild***, Thwaites ***Good Elf***, Woodforde's ***Great Eastern***, ***Wherry***, Norfolk Cider Co. ***Medium and Dry Ciders***

Fat Cat

49 West End Street, NR2 4NA. Telephone 01603 624364 – www.fatcatpub.co.uk
Gaffer Colin Keatley
Food: Rolls and pies when open.
Smoking Throughout – Open: 12 to 11, 12 to 12 Sat, 12 to 11 Sun

This is the ultimate, permanent street-corner real ale festival in a pub *'The only problem is that everyone else thinks it's the best pub in the world.'* (London Clarets) It is hard not to agree because this is the model for the future of top real ale houses. The chalk boards tell some of the story but the best tip is to spend an afternoon, watch the ales change and pick a theme for your drinking, ala real ale festival session. Then come again and do it all differently. It was deservedly CAMRA National pub of the Year 1998 and 2004.
UPDATE: Floss was her charming best as she told me of the new Fat Cat ales and Burnard's Cider. The Fat Cat name continues to expand.

BWV 21.9.04: Abbeydale ***Absolution***, Adnams ***Barley Mow***, ***Bitter***, ***Broadside***, ***Regatta***, ***Explorer***, Castle Rock ***Harvest Pale***, Enville Saaz ***Ginger Beer***, Hop Back ***Summer Lightning***, Fuller's ***ESB***, ***London Pride***, ***Organic Honey Dew***, Kelham Island ***Pale Rider***, Mauldons ***Mid Summer Gold***, Oakham ***Bishops Farewell***, Orkney ***Red McGregor***, Ridley's ***Old Bob***, Spectrum ***Wizard***, ***Rooster Cream***, Timothy Taylor ***Landlord*** , Woodforde's ***Wherry***
BWV 19.1.06: Adnams ***Bitter***, ***Old Ale***, Bateman ***Rosey Nosey***, Burton Bridge ***Golden Delicious***, ***Top Dog Stout***, Caledonian ***Deuchars IPA,*** Dave Winter's ***Tempest***, Elgood's ***Black Dog Mild***, Enville ***Ginger Ale***, Fat Cat ***Best Top Cat***, ***Stout***, Felinfoel ***Double Dragon***, Fuller's ***London Pride***, Grand Union ***Honey Porter***, Greene King ***Abbot***, Hop Back ***Summer Lightning***, Kelham Island ***Pale Rider***, Oakham ***Bishops Farewell***, Reedham ***Cherry Porter***, Shepherd Neame ***Spitfire***, Wadworth ***The Bishop's Tipple***, Woodforde's ***Nelson's Revenge***, ***Wherry***, Rum Cask ***Ciders***

The Shed

New

98 Lawson Road, NR3 4LF. Telephone 01603 413153
Gaffers Ryan and Diane Burnard
Food Filled rolls and pork pies 12 to 11, 11 to 11 Sat
No Smoking at Bar
Open: 12 to 11, 11 to 11 Sat

The Shed is the new kid on the real ale block but a novice it certainly is not. Opened in May 1995, it was a pub in its previous life. It has the traditions of its Banham and Fat Cat connections and a reputation for quality real ale. The building itself has been distinctively refurbished from its 60s design. The feeling is of a village hall/library/community club/folk club. They have their brewery on site, visible from the bar and it is obvious that live music makes a great impression on those who travel out from town to mix quality ale with their entertainment.

I just loved the place so much I had to return later. The pub continued to throw up surprises. The beautiful rosewood bar was apparently rescued from the shed in Banham from where the pub gets its name. Who, I wonder, lived in Evering Road, Hackney? Three ales rotate around their home brewery selections. Ryan brews the cider which certainly proves popular in the other pubs in this guide. And then there was Jude to make you feel at home when you chat at the bar.

BWV 19.1.06: Adnams ***Bitter***, ***Broadside***, Bateman ***Rosey Nosey***, Elgood's ***Black Dog Mild***, Green Jack ***Orange Wheat***, Harviestoun ***Bitter n'Twisted***, Fat Cat ***Black Cat Stout***, ***Fat Cat***, ***Santa Paws***, ***Top Cat***, Timothy Taylor ***Landlord***, Wadworth ***The Bishop's Tipple***, Burnard's ***Dry*** and ***Medium Ciders***

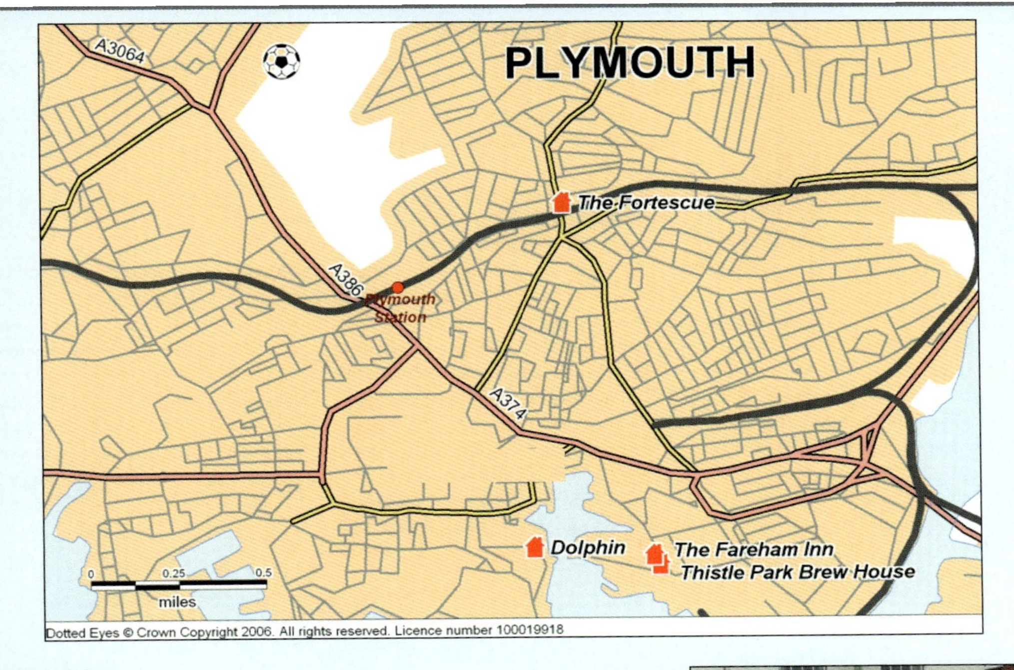

Dolphin

14 The Barbican, PL1 2LS. Telephone 01752 660876
Gaffer: William Holmes
Smoking Throughout MP TV
Open: 10 to 11 Mon to Thu, 10 to 12 Fri and Sat, 12 to 10.30 Sun

In total contrast to the Prince Maurice and refreshingly so, this pub is one that might, and perhaps never should, change. The Bass is legendary, served from the '*wood*' on the bar floor. It is beautifully basic despite its tourist location. I would choose this every time. The ships may have long gone but the Dolphin remains to remind us of port-side times past and long may it continue. I am told it is quite a haunt for Argyle celebrities on weekday evenings. It is one that I would make my destination on a walk around the rejuvenated Hoe. This is also the home of the Bosom Pals featuring Rick, in the Beryl Cook paintings that adorn the walls. My visit, one wet lunchtime, found easy conversation at the bar. Instantly, good recommendations were made for the best, and worst, of Plymouths' real ale pubs. Take their advice, avoid the fishy pubs on the hoe, geared up for tourist food, and settle into a quality time among locals and footie fans who make the extra effort to welcome friends and strangers to their quirky and distinctive watering hole.
UPDATE: If a pub hasn't changed in twenty years then why should it in the last?

BWV 11.2.05: Bass ***Draught***
BWV 30.5.06: Bass ***Draught***

The Fareham Inn

6 Commercial Road, PL4 0LD. Telephone 01752 201553
Gaffer: Veronica Caldwell
SmokingThroughout
Open: 11 to 11, 12 to 11 Sun

On the route from the Dolphin to the Thistle you will spot the Fareham. It looks like it has been recently renovated on the outside and shouts out that it is the cosiest pub in Plymouth.

So it was that on a typically damp day in December I found the hospitality of Ronnie and her locals along with my mates being dragged along for the fun of it. Ronnie has been here for eleven years and served up a great pint of St. Austell Cousin Jack. I was not the only footie fan to find it, as it is well known by the discerning traveller. Oh for more space at the bar to get a wider range, but it is just not possible in this small and indeed comfortable, street-corner boozer. The pub has a good pub feeling. The locals are likely to be fishermen and/or Albion rugger types rather than back-street footie fans. The walls were timbered, the floors flag-stoned. It didn't take long to get into conversation about ale and the fact that the single ale rotates regularly, usually from regional independent brewers, and what's more, at a rarely found realistic price! Next time it will be a pint of Summerskills and, if it is an evening session, the locals will be in full pub game mode; darts, board games and euchre, being popular. The Fareham is a great little pub and well located for the inevitable renovation of the nearby dockyards that has just started.

BWV 31.12.05: St Austell ***Cousin Jack***

The Fortescue

New

37 Mutley Plain, PL4 6JR. Telephone 01752 660673
Gaffer: Steve Smith
Food: Sunday lunch 12 to 3.30
Smoking Throughout
11 to 11 Mon to Sat, 12 to 10.30 Sun

Mutley Plain will be well known by students of the town ands is the nearest suburban village to Home Park. The Fortescue is a good example of how in the nineties some locals were redesigned to create traditional style pubs that stand the test of time and remain as places that should now be cherished.

Steve, the landlord is himself a Wolves fan and is keen to welcome real ale drinking away fans to his pub. They will find a long bar that runs the length of a narrow room and a small snug. Outside is a great decked patio for pavement-gazing and downstairs a cellar bar that doubles as *'The Acoustic café.'* The music theme gives a clue to the atmosphere in the pub. It is a pub for a wide range of people but the common denominator is good ale and quality entertainment. The local bands play regularly, often four in a night. The juke box certainly met with the approval of this lunchtime visitor, no chance of Eurovision songs being played here. The pub is one for good banter. The room is arranged with large bench seats around which to share a pint, a game of cards or, as they did on my visit, read the local papers. The pub is literally highly polished and well cared for, so too the beers. The pub notice board gives a better clue to its community function. Next week they are off to watch cricket at Taunton. The pub teams appear to be social teams as they play a lot of pub sports without winning very much.

BWV 30.5.06: Bass ***Draught***, Greene King ***Abbot***, Hydes ***Jekyll's Gold***, Tom Wood ***Hop and Glory***, Thwaites ***Bomber***

Prince Maurice

3 Church Hill, Eggbuckland PC6 SRJ. Telephone 01752 771515
Gaffer: Rick Dodds
Food: Good value weekday bar snacks 12 to 2.30
Separate smoking areas
Open: 11 to 3, 7 to 11 Mon to Thu, 11 to 11 Fri and Sat, 12 to 10.30 Sun

This near perfect hillside village local is located in a commuter village just outside of town and has a character to die for. Open log fires, good views, bucket loads of character and great ales. It does get very busy both when Argyle and the Albion play. I was diverted on my visit by the Titanic pictures, the locals' crossword for charity and the chat of the regulars. It is a comfortable; bring your dog and paper, type of place at lunchtime. Patently in the centre of village life, the Prince Maurice also has plenty of regulars who make the journey out from Plymouth seeking a bit of country life and an easy journey home. Six regular ales are the norm supplemented by two ever changing local guest ales and for travelling fans that means new beers to sup from Devon and Cornwall.
UPDATE: The pub was totally unchanged and had the same characters in the pub when I visited this year.

BWV 11.2.05: Adnams ***Broadside***, Badger ***Tanglefoot***, Cains ***Raisin***, Courage ***Best***, East St. ***Cream***, Randall's ***Patois VB***, Summerskills ***Best***, Thatcher's ***Cider***, Valley ***Cider***
BWV 30.5.06: Adnams ***Broadside***, Burton Bridge ***Spring Ale***, Courage ***Best***, Greene King ***Old Speckled Hen***, St. Austell ***HSB***, Sharp's ***Doom Bar***, Summerskills ***Best***, ***FFB***

Thistle Park Brew House

32 Commercial Road, PL4 OLE. Telephone 01752 204890
Gaffers: Quentin and Debbie Style
Food: All home -cooked, freshly sourced menu with a South African twist 12 to 10
Smoking Throughout
Open: 12 to 2 am Mon to Sat, 12 to 1 am Sun

This is a unique refurbishment by the rugby loving, ale brewing, South African landlord. A street corner locals that is popular with all age ranges at different times of the day. It has two very different rooms; the larger bar has large drinking space and tables for group sessions. The smaller, darker, standing-room only bar, reminded me of a University bar that is easily transformed into music venue/meeting space. It is a '*nouveau spit and sawdust pub offering urban chic to locals and businessmen alike*.' I would walk across water to find this pub, no don't, it is better to use the footbridge from the Hoe instead.
UPDATE: The pub was being rebuilt/refurbished when I visited this year and the plans for the pub are truly impressive. They include creating a restaurant and roof garden, larger bar frontage for more ale choices, a new entrance, street tables and more room to enjoy this great pub. The orange room is finished. Music and sports plays a full part in making this the most popular real ale pub in the town centre.

BWV 11.2.05: South Hams ***Brewery Bitter***, Sutton ***Eddystone***, ***Pandamonium***, ***Plymouth Pride***, ***XSB***

BWV 30.5.06: South Hams ***Eddystone***, ***Wild Blonde***, Sutton ***Plymouth Porter***, ***Plymouth Pride***, ***XSB***

Plymouth

A surprisingly big place, that is probably the longest away trip for most visiting teams, although it is not a place many travelling fans seem to look forward to as an overnight adventure. In terms of attractions there are lots of interesting things to see in and around Plymouth; some even like the 60's architecture that replaced the Luftwaffe flattened centre; there are exciting developments; and Cornwall is the other side of the river Tamar. On the other hand, thanks to the docks and Navy, Plymouth, was always a working town full of transitory workers from around the country; which could make finding a bed for the night difficult. The tale of sleeping on a rain lashed bowling green after been turned away by the Youth Hostel with the overflowing car park is waiting to be told.

Plymouth Hoe

This is basically a long grassy hump by a cliff; and if you walk up to it from the old town, one of our finest seascapes hoves into your view as you breast the ridge. Plymouth Sound lies below, with a Royal Navy ship cutting through it if you are lucky. There are wooded hills and islands on both sides; and the Atlantic beyond the spectacular Breakwater; which was built between 1812-1844 to stop ship breaking waves from south-westerly Atlantic gales roaring right up the Sound. The Hoe is home to Smeaton's Tower, the Eddystone lighthouse from 1759-1882, and a Maritime museum called the Dome.

Preston

The Priest-town is ancient, and is proud with some reason. It grew rich on cotton, yet avoided the reputation for soul crushing grimness of many mill towns.

The Harris Museum and Art Gallery

This is one of the best of its kind in England, and shows other northern towns that museums can reflect a place's pride.

The National Football Museum

Well worth a visit, but it struck us as being designed by some cappuccino swilling, marketing stain on the bed sheet of humanity, who thinks they understand what the 'real football experience' is, but never actually pays to experience it. It used to boast about an interactive display where: 'Gabby Yorath, Jimmy Hill and Mark Lawrenson share their expertise.' We don't want their expertise! We want to interactively attack TV pundits. That would pull in real fans!

St Walburga's Church

This stunning Victorian church, has the country's tallest parish spire. There is an ancient tradition of sending Walburga cards on the 25th February. It started in 1985 when Glyn Watkins forgot to send a Valentine: so he got a Saints book and picked Walburga as Patron Saint of the forgetful, because he liked the name. It turned out she was an Anglo-Saxon. She and her brothers, St Willibald and St Winnibald, helped convert the Germans to Christianity. She later became Abbess of one of Europe's most important monasteries, but unlike Hildergard of Bingen she never wrote tunes or descriptions of her libido, so modern fashion has passed her by.

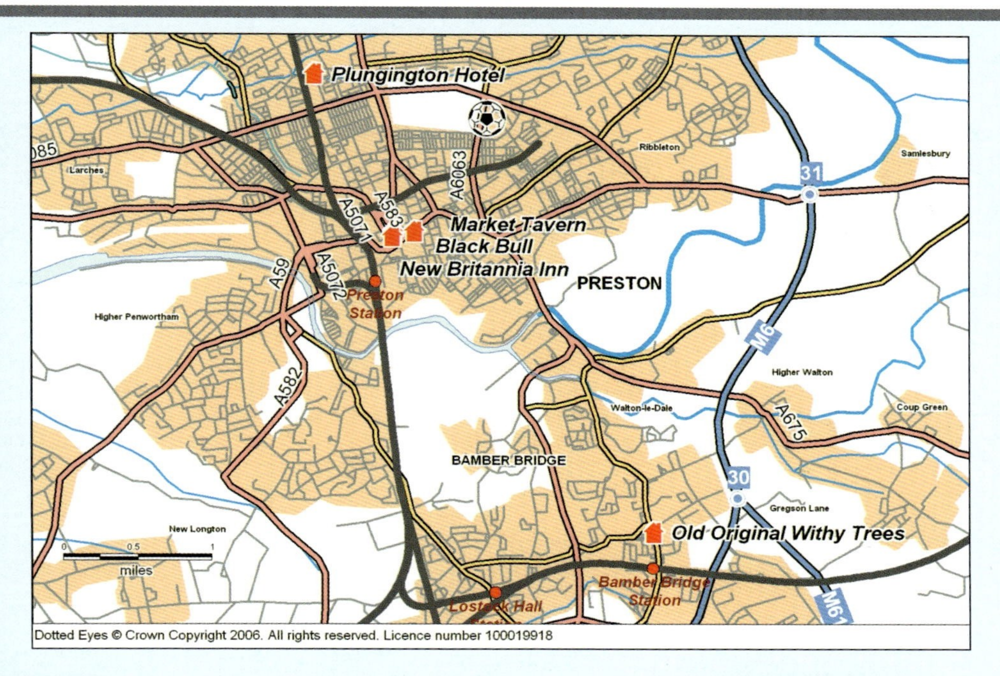

Black Bull

35 Friargate, PR1 2AT. Telephone 01772 823397
Gaffer: Stan Eaton
No smoking at the bar
Open: 10.30 to 11

Stan has been landlord at the Black Bull for 15 years and the pub has a great reputation for both ales and the quality of the atmosphere to be found. Nine ales are always on sale and seven of those will be rotating from a long list of regional and local beers. The beer choice reflects the local taste for lighter bitters rather than dark porters.

The Bull has a prime location yet is truly a regulars' haunt. Wetherspoons may be directly opposite but they occupy quite different worlds as far as clientele are concerned. The pub is deceptively large, extending deep to the rear from its timber-framed and tiled frontage. Standing room is plentiful in the bar area but, more comfortably, the pub has several snugs for more intimate sessions.

Stan is an Everton fan who is well aware of the footie and real ale scene. The place has a busy buzz on a match-day, which is matched by more noise when Preston are in their regular play-off action on the big screen. The Black Bull is part of the local papers' real ale crawl and it provides contrast to its equally good ale pub next door, not included here.

BWV 11.10.05: Cains ***Bitter***, Boddingtons ***Bitter***, Darwin ***Rolling Hitch***, Fernandes ***Cask Master Bitter***, Hart ***Temptress***, Leyden ***Raglan Sleeve***, Marston's ***Pedigree***, Staffordshire ***Special***, Wood ***Special***

PRESTON NORTH END

Market Tavern

33-35 Market Street, PR1 2ES. Telephone 01772 254425
Gaffer: Tracey Hodgson
No food but welcome to bring your own
Smoking Throughout
Open: 10.30 to 11 Thu to Sat, 10.30 to 9 Mon to Wed, 12 to 9 Sun

This busy Preston CAMRA pub of the year (2004) is a comfortable multi-sectioned retreat from the bustle of Friargate and the nearby market. Tracey sets a fine example of how serving quality ales will help to create a friendly pub without the need for pretension. As George Hartley says '*the excellent staff take pride in what they do.*' '*The best for alternative ales*' (RA Jones of Preston) The chalk-board records 256 ales so far this year and rarely are they repeated, so it is well worth going here just for the surprises it can offer. My visit was a very refreshing change from other, perhaps more famous, nearby Preston pubs who found it difficult to recognise that every customer is important. In true Northern style one punter said '*take your missus with you and she can shop at the brilliant market whilst you enjoy the beer. It is so good that we always go back for more and usually the beer has changed again.*' (Phil P) The welcome at The Market Tavern session made for an excellent hour well spent. *UPDATE*: 361 different beers by visiting date this year.

BWV 22.11.04: Brains ***Rev James***, Cains ***Traditional Bitter***, Wessex ***Banger***
BWV 11.10.05: Bateman's ***Valiant***, Brakspear ***Hop Demon***, Mordue ***Workie Ticket***, Young's ***Old Nick***

New Britannia Inn

6 Heatley Street, PR1 2XB. Telephone 01772 253424
Gaffer: Nick Robinson
Food: Home-made pub food 11.30 to 2
Smoking Throughout
Open: 11 to 11, 12 to 10.30 Sun

This is an excellent one-room, low-ceilinged, Victorian bar that has a fantastic and ever-changing range of ales. Within walking distance of the station and town centre, yet in a side street, the New Britannia has a great name among the punters in the other real ale pubs in the town. This is a top-notch boozer that has a deserved reputation for offering a range of ales to suit all drinking preferences. It is very easy to get into friendly conversation, the locals being very helpful in talking about the quality, or not, of the Preston match-day experience. The list of ales is drawn from near and far, but my eye was drawn to the choice of rarer northern brews. Unfortunately the food is not available on Saturdays.
UPDATE: Preston CAMRA Pub of the Year 2005. New ownership: Nick has taken over from Paula and the good news is that it is in very safe hands. Beer festivals are planned for March and November.

BWV 22.11.04: Boddingtons ***Bitter***, Bronte ***Derwent***, Flowers ***IPA***, Goose Eye ***Parsons Pledge***, Marstons ***Pedigree***, Phoenix ***Porter***, Saxon ***Ruby Tuesday Cider***
BWV 11.10.05: Boddingtons ***Bitter***, Blythe ***Tamworth Special***, ***Castle Eden Ale***, Goose Eye ***Bronte Bitter***, Isle of Mull ***The Terror of Tobermoray***, Salamander ***Holy Roller***, Shardlow ***Golden Miles***, Wylam ***Houblon Nouveau***, Saxon ***Greensleeves Cider***

Old Original Withy Trees

157 Station Road, Bamber Bridge, PR5 6LA. Telephone 01772 330396
Gaffers: Bob and Jane Burns
Smoking Throughout
Open: 11 to 11, 12 to 10.30 Sun

CP SKY BM PG

The Old Original is an old farm-house, set back from the main old A6. It is big and roomy with unusual features such as a great beer garden and separate drinking spaces in traditional pub style. The quality of the beers and the general atmosphere reflect the family pride of the landlord and his wife. If you get the same friendliness as I found then the locals will make you very welcome. It was well worth a return visit on the way out of town, returning to the same conversations of earlier in the day. It is relatively close to the motorway making it ideal for the fans who want a pub well away from the ground yet not in town. A beer in the garden, a chat at the bar, a meeting place to organise a taxi to the ground, all would be fine here. Buses do run into town, as does the local railway.
UPDATE: It was refurbished before being taken over by W+D. The pub retains its village-local character and is as popular as ever. Not, however, with the CAMRA guide compilers – well, what do they know? On beer quality and being a great local it will always be in my guide.

BWV 22.11.04: Archers ***SSB***, Burtonwood ***Bitter***
BWV 11.10.05: Banks's ***Bitter***, Jennings ***Sneck Lifter***, Marston's ***Pedigree***

The Plungington Hotel

67 Lytham Road, Fulwood, PR2 3AR. Telephone 01772 787081
Gaffer: Anthony Quinn
Separate smoking areas
Open: 12 to 11

SP SKY JB PG D

The search for a pub nearer the ground led me around the ring road to nearby Fulwood and the new home of Tony, the former landlord of the Stanley in town. The pub has a undergone a classic refurbishment and has a traditional, but updated, hotel bar feel. This includes distinctive bar and lounge and as a top draw, (and drawer) a Bowling Green. Make sure Darcy, the dog, stays off it though!

As you might imagine, the pub is at the heart of the local community, offering a proper games room that has lost its space invaders to the lounge. Everything is on a grand scale yet it remains intimate rather than aircraft-hangar in style. It was good to hear the history of the pub and the Tanners windows and talk footie life with some locals, even if it was of Manchester Utd and their troubles, bless!

The pub is a bus ride from town (No 22/23) and a twenty minute walk to the ground – this is probably quicker than a bus or taxi as the crowds build up. Given the parking issue it would be a great stopping-off point to guarantee a post-match return, which is what many away fans often do.

BWV 11.10.05: Everards ***Equinox***, ***Tiger***, Fuller's ***London Pride***, Greene King ***Old Speckled Hen***, Theakston ***Bitter***

Crown and Sceptre

34 Holland Road, West Kensington, W14 8BA. Telephone 020 7602 1866
Gaffers: Jenny, Phil and Dominic Walker
Food: Excellent home made menu with authentic Mexican variations to the Bristish fayre 12 to 9.30
Separate smoking areas
Open: 11 to 11 Mon to Fri, 12 to 11 Sun

The '*Celebrated Crown and Sceptre*' is such a welcome find that entering it you instantly get a feeling that reality has returned and the West London experience can be put to the back of the mind, never to be visited again. It is instantly refreshing, modern yet with proper pub values, a good place to visit and somewhere to come to again.

The pub is a street corner pub in the heart of the Kensington Range Rover run. It consists of one bar split into different sections by carefully placed farmhouse style tables and settees. The back of the bar has a raised area complete with open fire and all is decorated in the '*Changing Rooms*' choice of Terracotta and Cherry. I liked the comfort, the way that one could easily keep your conversations to oneself or alternatively get involved in larger party activities when that is desired, I chatted with Jenny and instantly felt that there is a genuine friendship extended to those who love real ale and good food. It is not really a football pub; it is too genteel for that. This is a place for young couples, those locals who have a nanny to sample an ale and chat of the house in the country. The beer is constantly rotating; they have sold 281 different beers in four years on just three pulls. The pub is busiest on those long Friday nights; quietest when the thirty-something's have retired to the Cotswolds for the weekend. Lunchtime has Universal workers enjoying the interesting alternative menu.

BWV 17.5.06: Acorn ***Darkness***, Frog Island ***Bitter***, Young's ***Special***

The Green

172 Uxbridge Road, Shepherds Bush, W12 2JP. Telephone 020 8749 5709

New

Gaffer: Rebecca Blackmore

Food: Good value modern pub food in the '*Smith and Jones*' style 12 to 9

Smoking Throughout

Open: 12 to 11 Mon to Thu, 12 to 11.30 Fri and Sat, 12 to 10.30 Sun

F

MP SKY D

The recommendation for the Green came from a regional pub manager who suggested this is a great pub for pre-match pint and banter. It has a very easy to find location. It is on the NW corner of Shepherds Bush Green, on the natural route to the ground. It consists of one room that is big enough to hold large groups, yet it has discrete sections where getting one more than two to sit together is something of a challenge. It also has a largish function room complete with table football table and a sign that says it might be booked for VIP Sport sessions!

I chatted with Lyn, the Scottish Rangers fan who described her regulars as very friendly. The lunch time trade consists of a curious mix of lads in Rangers leisure wear, couples enjoying a liquid lunch and single women, escaping perhaps, from the BBC canteen. The conversation was very much football related, the European Cup Final was due to be screened later that day and this would be perfect, as all parts of the pub had a screen in view. The pub is very much a QPR pub. It has some great pictures of Stan Bowles and other legends behind the bar and a team flag is draped over the fire among those ready for the world cup. It will be friendly on match days and is well used to having mixed groups of fans. The beer choice was good; usually there are five ever rotating choices. It is indeed the closest good ale choice to the ground

BWV 17.5.06: Archers ***IPA***, ***Town Crier***, Fuller's ***Discovery***, ***London Pride***

Radnor Arms

247 Warwick Road, Kensington, W14 8PX. Telephone 020 7602 7708

New

Gaffers: Peter and Trudy Lambert

You are welcome to bring in take-aways and sandwiches

Smoking Throughout

Open: 12 to 11 Mon to Fri, 5.30 to 11.30 Sat to Sun

B

The Radnor has a special place in my heart, as it was here that I had the pre book-launch pint last year. It should also be important in the thoughts of many who want to save pubs from the whims of developers masquerading as Insurance Companies. It is under threat of closure and I make no apologies in urging you to see for yourself why the petition to save it should be supported.

The pub internal design is gloriously different. On first entering you will notice a splash of colour from the fish tank that lies in what might be termed the '*Stage room*.' This small and cosy room hosts the TV screen and is decked out in genuine rugby collectables. The other end of the bar is like the kitchen of a country house complete with dresser that has a beer bottle collection. In between is the main bar, is a space that would make a perfect village bar.

It comes complete with a notice to '*beware of the pussy*.' The Ginger cat will be curled up by the tank, Splodge will be roaming, and looking for trouble. Peter and Trudy have returned here and run a really friendly pub. The trade relies on two ever changing guest ales and, rare for London, an appropriate Tiger. Local office workers and of course Olympia escapees are often found in the pub playing board games. The age range is varied, young on a Tuesday elderly on a Sunday night, generally in the forties. It has been recommended and visited by real ale fans over the years and makes a great alternative to the lager bars on the High Street nearby.

BWV 17.5.06: Everards ***Tiger***, Sharp's ***Eden***, Spinning Dog ***Chase the Tail***

Queens Park Rangers

QPR play in Shepherds Bush. It is not recorded who the shepherd was, or what he did with the bush, but it was clearly marginal land; you keep sheep on land not good enough for corn or cows. This marginality has lasted to modern times and is why Shepherds Bush is famous for things no sensible person would want to associate with, like Steptoe and Son's scrapyard in Oil Drum Lane, Wormwood Scrubs Prison, and the BBC Television Centre. One of these three may not be the home of warped people living bitter lives, but that is only because Oil Drum Lane never existed.

'He smelt of pubs and Wormwood Scrubs'
Down in the tube station at midnight ***The Jam***

The Scrubs

The prison was built by convict labour between 1875 and 1891. The front gate is of architectural interest, has portraits of the prison reformers Elizabeth Fry and John Howard, and featured in several films, including The Italian Job. There is a large area of common land behind the prison which was famous for dueling and is now a nature reserve, although we do not know if the snakes the area was named after are back.

White City

Named after a vanished stadium and exhibition area built for the 1908 Olympics. It is one of the grounds Queens Park ranged through, and was built to time and budget, which young readers may find as unbelievable as wet leather footballs with the weight of solid wood.

Sheffield Wednesday

The worst thing about visiting Sheffield is the way the centre was cut off from the rail and bus stations by one of the worst concrete creations in England, with one dank, foul and dark subway as the only link. While most of Sheffield now looks better than we ever remember it, the concrete barrier remains: but at least there is a tram stop above the station, even if it is as appallingly signposted as everything else there.

Supertram

While motorists may dream of happy days BST (Before SuperTram) when Sheffield had fewer trenches than the Somme of 1916, and driving through it did not involve being stationary or trapped in the one way system for weeks. For pedestrians however it is a wonder. You can even park your car at Meadowhall and catch a tram to Hillsborough.

Industrial Museum

Kelham Island is now called Abbeydale Industrial Hamlet and the Industrial Museum is officially called Kelham Island Museum. We do not think they are calling a spade a person energised extractive facilitating device, yet. Industrial museums reminds us of when Britain had an industry other than leisure. Sheffield's was grimy and smelled like a factory. We once recommended visiting before it was made as clean as a corporate raider's conscience, but it may be too late now. The museum still has a awesome Bessemer steel convertor to see outside, but that is about all you will see on Friday's and Saturday's because it is shut, apparently after consultations with experts about falling visitor numbers.

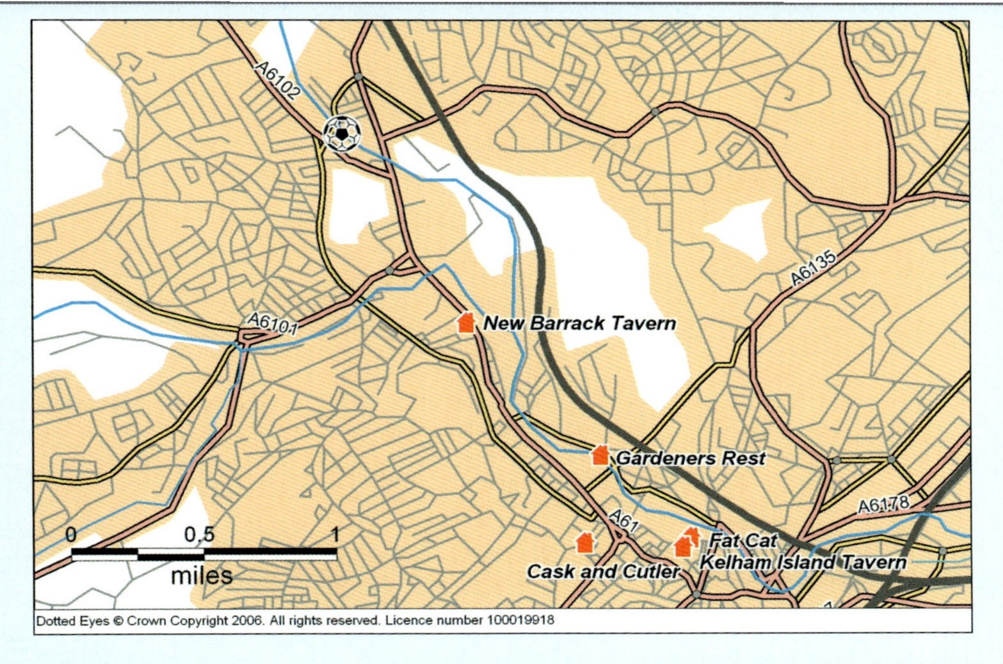

Cask and Cutler

1 Henry Strteet, S3 7EQ. Telephone 0114 2492295
Gaffer: Neil Clarke
Separate smoking areas
Open: 5.30 to 11 Mon, 12 to 2, 5.30 to 11 Tue to Thu, 12 to 11 Fri and Sat, 12 to 3, 7 to 10.30 Sun, 12 to 3, 5.30 to 11 Bank Holiday Mon

The most recommended of the local pubs the Cask and Cutler is located at the end of the local Shalemoor tram stop. Or conversely Gary S of Sheffield says '*it offers a constantly changing range of excellently kept real ales within staggering distance of the tram stop taking you to the Mecca of football – Hillsborough.*' Dynamic, yet traditional, small but large of heart, I would challenge anyone not to think this pub is perfectly formed. The two rooms are equally private, being screened by the internal walls and woodwork. The pubs offers unusual ales that constantly change plus Belgian bottled ales. Nicola S of Barnsley has it right, '*It keeps my husband occupied with the plethora of real ales whilst I hit the shops*!' There are no themes or music, just regulars chatting or planning an evening that, on my visit, involved bringing a bottle to carry home the ale.
UPDATE: Ring to check out the beers on at the Mid Nov beer festival

BWV 12.5.06: Archer's ***King's Shilling***, Boggart Hole Clough ***Darwin***, Durham ***Spring Goddess***, Glentworth ***Gold n'Light***, Hart ***Cait-lin Gold***, Lancaster ***LM***, Marston Moor ***Spring Hatch***, Pictish ***Maelstrom***, Port Mahon ***Ryan's Daughter***, Weston's ***Scrumpy***
BWV 14.3.05: E+S ***Old Gimmer***, Hart ***Cartford***, Pictish ***Brewers Gold***, Whitley Bridge ***Bridge Gold***, ***Emberzale***, Millstone ***Windy Miller***, Salamander ***Stout***, Weston's ***Old Rosie Cider***

MP SKY D

Fat Cat

23 Alma Road, S3 8SA Telephone 0114 2494801
www.thefatcat.co.uk
Gaffer: David Wickett
Food: Good quality home cooked food with special vegetarian, vegan and gluten free options 12 to 2.30, 6 to 7.30 Mon to Fri, 12 to 2.30 Sat and Sun
Separate smoking areas
Open: 12 to 11 Mon to Thu, sometimes extended.
12 to 12 Fri and Sat, 12 to 11 Sun

This is the most quaint and original of the three Fat Cats in these guides As the Kelham Island tap room alone it would gain a national fame without the name. It is a tiny pub with two small rooms, one being quite separate and smoke free. Both have a highly polished and well cared for quality, suggesting that the comfort of the punters is as important as the high quality and diverse ales. Add in a distinctive menu and you have a pub that appeals to couples in their middle ages as well as the older crew found in traditional ale houses. The leader of the Sheffield revolution it has managed to maintain the highest of standards as the numerous awards testify. This is a great pub that has a must not miss element.
UPDATE: Sky will available in the upstairs function room. Beer festivals to look out for in August, December and May. The pictures went with the refurbished toilets.

BWV 12.5.06: Cottage ***SS Great Britain***, Derby ***Phenomenal***, Derwent ***Springtime***, Kelham Island ***Best***, ***Pale Rider***, Northumberland ***Ashington Ale***, Scattor Rock ***Meadow Mild***, Thornbridge ***Blackthorn Ale***, Timothy Taylor ***Landlord***, Saxon ***Cider***
BWV 14.3.05: Acorn ***Legend***, Cottage ***Evening Star***, Fat Cat ***Bitter***, Durham ***Nine Stars***, Hart ***Cartford Premium***, Kelham Island ***Pale Rider***, ***Best***, ***Easy Rider***, Salamander ***Blunderbus***

SP PG D

Gardeners Rest

105 Neepend Lane, S3 3AT Telephone 0114 2724978
Gaffers: Pat Wilson and Eddy Munnelly
Separate smoking areas
Open: 3 to 11 Mon to Thu, 12 to 11 Fri and Sat, 12 to 10.30 Sun

And so to my personal favourite in the Sheffield crawl. Instantly the locals made it obvious that this was a pub for those who value matters local in ale and life. They offer regular ales, ever changing guests, ale selection on gravity and ciders. I once was a Geographer so I went into the conservatory that has planning maps to find a view of the Don undergoing its rejuvenation. In the bar I claimed my place on the map over the bar. Soon it became a conversation with Tim, author of the guide to Sheffield pubs and the tour of the area could easily have ended here as the warmth of the place was just perfect. The front snug is quite separate from the rest of the pub. The ultimate accolade came when local brewers came in for a pint. The People of Sheffield don't know just how lucky they are.
UPDATE: The Garden Work in Progress may be finished next year, by the October Beer Festival?

BWV 12.5.06: Blakemere ***Wigwam***, Bradfield ***Farmers IPA***, Leyden ***Wheelwright***, Naylor's ***Erica's Ginger Roots***, Timothy Taylor ***Golden Best***, ***Landlord***, Wentworth ***Gun Park Dark Mild***, ***WPA***,
BWV 14.3.05: Bowland ***Malmsey Butt***, Greenfield ***Pride Of England***, ***Castleshaw***, Houston's ***Horny Wee Devil***, Timothy Taylor ***Landlord***, ***Best***, ***Golden Best***, Wentworth ***Needle's Eye***, Weston's ***Old Rosie***, Herefordshire ***Country Perry***

Kelham Island Tavern

62 Russell Street, S3 8RW. Telephone 0114 2722482
www.kelhamislandtavern.co.uk
Gaffer: Trevor Wraithe
Food: Traditional bar snacks and full menu 12 to 3 Tue to Sat
Separate smoking areas
Open: 12 to 11 Mon to Sat, 12 to 3, 7 to 11 Sun

The local pub of the year is the obvious starting point for the Kelham Island crawl. There is a danger you might not leave though. It is a spotless haunt of the chattering classes and my visit soon found the locals in full flow, topics ranging from politics to mediaeval history. The pub extends backwards into the courtyard where the reason for the Yorkshire in Bloom awards becomes evident in the small garden. The pub has a classy style, festooned with classic art work and classic ale choices. It is a top boozer that all will enjoy a beautiful bar with beautiful beer. The pub is rightly a regular beer award winner; one cannot be less impressed by not only the range of ales, but their quality. *UPDATE*: Check the website for beers and festivals. Local CAMRA POTY 2006

BWV 12.5.06: Acorn ***Barnsley Bitter***, Archers ***Full Time***, Bartrams ***Best***, Derby ***Little Gem***, ***Phenomenal***, Durham ***White Amarillo***, Mauldon's ***Suffolk Comfort***, Mighty Oak ***Shamrock Stout***, Otley ***O1***, Pictish ***Brewer's Gold***, Thornbridge ***Kastor***
BWV 14.3.05 Acorn ***Barnsley Bitter***, Archers ***Predator***, Arkells ***3B***, Glentworth ***Yorkshire Light Ale***, Leydon ***On me head son***!, Ossett ***Silver King***, Pictish ***Brewers Gold***, Rudgate ***Happy Masher***, Saxon ***Ruby Tuesday***, ***Platinum Blonde***, Weston's ***Old Rosie Cider***

New Barrack Tavern

New

601 Penistone Road, S6 2GA. Telephone 0144 2211689
Gaffers: Kevin and Stephanie Woods
Food: A wide choice of good simple, wholesome pub food
11 to 3, 5 to 9 Mon to Thu, 11 to 12 Fri and Sat, 12 to 11 Sun
Smoking Throughout
Open: 12 to 3, 7 to 11 Mon to Sat, 12 to 3, 7.30 to 11 Sun

Tynemill pubs always offer a great beer range in pleasant proper pub environments The knowledgeable folk of Sheffield said the guide had no value without this pub being included so being one to take the pleasurable route I braved the Penistone Rd traffic to take a photo and settled down for a perfect mid afternoon pint.

The pub has three very different rooms plus an excellent standing at the bar space. The small snug doubled as a darts area when I visited. The large lounge found groups of friends enjoying a regular sampling exploration in a room with tobacco and beer posters for decoration. The conservatory to the rear is the non smoking room, and guess what, it was as popular as every smoke free room in the country The standing bar space was crowded and it was soon obvious that this is the preferred location for the locals and regulars, the football fans and post work story tellers. On match days you will need to get here very early, it will be very busy. Kevin and the locals are very welcoming and well versed in the popularity of this classic real ale ticker destination. The beer board also lists masses of continental draught ales and bottled beers. No hassle is guaranteed, this is indeed a great pub.

BWV 12.5.06: Abbeydale ***Moonshine***, Acorn ***Barnsley Bitter***, Badger ***Tanglefoot***, Burton Bridge ***Flying Fun***, Castle Rock ***Elsie Mo***, ***Harvest Pale***, Cropton ***Balmy Mild***, HB Clark's ***Black Mild***, Springhead ***Puritan's Porter***, Wellington ***Entirely Porter***

FOOTBALL AND REAL ALE GUIDE

PREMIERSHIP PUB OF THE YEAR

As voted for by the readers 2006-07

The Anvil

Dorning St, Wigan

BWV 1.3.05: Hydes *Anvil*, *Dark Mild*. Merlin *Cannonball*, Phoenix *Arizona*, Rooster's *Yankee*

BWV 5.6.06: Hydes *Bitter*, *Mild*, Phoenix *Arizona*, Rooster's *Yankee*

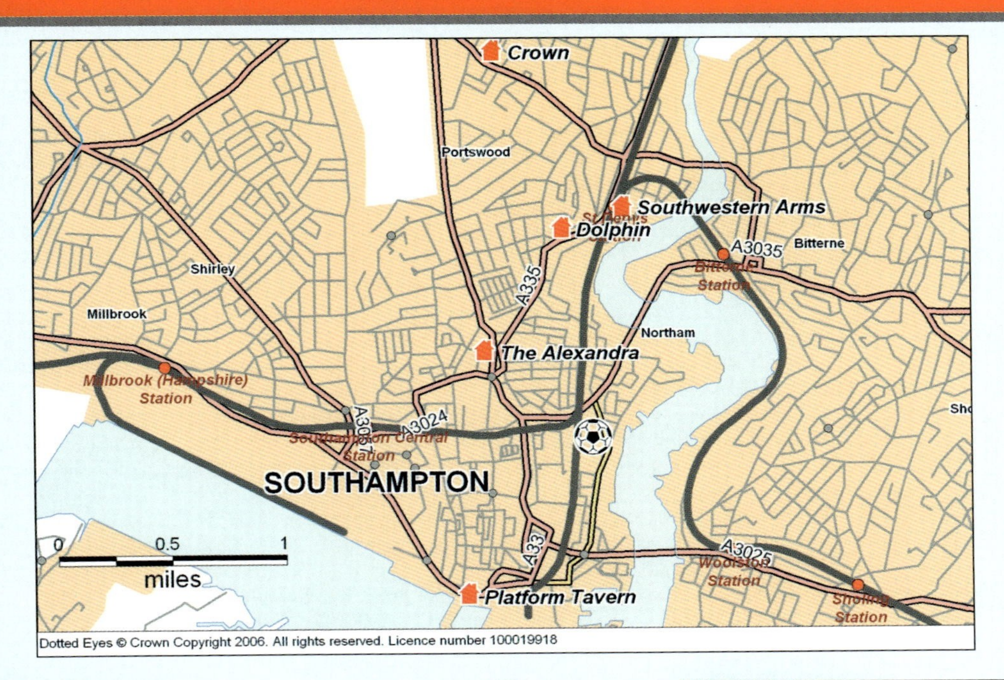

The Alexandra

New

6 Bellevue Road, SO15 2AY. Telephone 023 80 335071
Gaffer: Joe Khalil
Food: Good quality pub-food, speciality chilli chips, 12 to 3
Separate smoking areas
Open: 11 to 11, 12 to 10.30 Sun

If, like me, a visit to Southampton must take in a visit to the old Dell haunts of Bedford Place and London Road, then you will soon find that the previously-great pub area is struggling to keep its real ale. The Alexandra is the exception and has managed to maintain matchday traditions for home and away fans and it also has a location that is relatively useful for those trekking from the Station to St. Mary's.

The pub has been recently renovated to become a large open-plan pub with some nice real pub touches, such as the table football at the rear, traditional tiles and large Victorian furniture that complements the high hotel-style ceilings. Joe has moved in, and the real ale choices remain. Guest ale rotates from the Punch list and suits those locals, '*the beardy, weirdy brigade*' who make up the regular customers. On my visit it was office-workers and students. The pub only becomes a footie pub in the hours before and after the match. It is well-known among premiership away fans that hold it in great regard. It is a large, real pub with real fires and very comfortable. It was near one such fire I settled to my pint and reflectively gazed out of the large picture window, planning the best route to walk to the stadium.

BWV 4.1.06: Fuller's ***London Pride***, Ringwood ***Best***, Shepherd Neame ***Spitfire***, Timothy Taylor ***Landlord***

Crown

8 Highcrown Street, Highfield SO17 1QE. Telephone 023 80315033
Gaffer: Jacquie Hahyer
Food: Different menus lunchtime and evening, something for all tastes from traditional fish and chips to steaks, 12 to 2.15, 6 to 9.30, 6 to 10 Fri and Sat, 7 to 10 Sun
Smoking Throughout
Open: 11 to 11, 12 to 11 Sun.

I must confess to being very surprised by the changes made at the Crown. Having said that, one of my University locals of 20+ years ago, was one that I would have expected to have gone the way of so many ale houses. It is one large bar, decorated in country pub style, but keeping the feel of a locals' bar with areas set aside for conversation and pub games. '*It draws a mix of locals and academics* (CAMRA 2004) *Beware it could have 50% more capacity and still be full on weekends*!' On my visit it was the academics and locals who filled the pub, a great atmosphere prevailed as groups of regulars got stuck into great lunchtime pub food and quality ale. Chatty, and obviously popular with all ages and both sexes, the pub also has a heated outside patio for those long summer evenings when the student grant needs careful handling. For me it fits the bill as a place to avoid the congestion of the city centre.
UPDATE Uli Pfeifer runs the pub for Steve and Jacquie, they having tailored the food to their local clientele. The pub goes from strength to strength, retaining a great relaxed atmosphere.

BWV 24.8.04: Bass ***Draught***, Flowers ***Original***, Fuller's ***London Pride***, Ringwood ***Best Bitter***, Strong's ***Best***
BWV 4.1.06: Bass ***Draught***, Flowers ***Original***, Fuller's ***London Pride***, Ringwood ***Best***, Strong's ***Best***

Dolphin

New

30 Osborne Road South, SO17 2EX. Telephone 02380 399369
Gaffers: Chris and Sandie Shakespeare
Food: Locally supplied food prepared and cooked to order. (Phone in advance for larger groups) 12 to 2.30, 6.30 to 8.30
Separate smoking areas CP BM
Open: 12 to 11, 12 to 10.30 Sun.

Should you take the route westward from St. Denys Station you will see the pub garden of the Dolphin from the footbridge. What a great find this pub is and what a great set of folk you will meet when you go in for a pint or two. Timbered throughout and with great log fires, it is the epitome of cosy and atmospheric. Add in a dollop of blues as live music or even on a Sunday the landlord leading the live music sessions, then you might come a little closer to the true Dolphin experience. Then one notices quirky posters by a local graphic artist, the access to the cellar slap is bang in the middle of the bar and then one starts to doubt the advertised beer strength. And so it was that I finished my search for the best that the Bevois valley area has with this great pub, definitely a real pub, but with the added bonus of Sandies' great food. The trains will rattle by if in summer you use the garden. On a footie visit I would definitely pre book a taxi and do the two pubs either side of the station. If you fancy a longer crawl the Bevois Castle and New Inn are pretty close as well, but why move on when the range of ales will suit most person's needs for a variety pack session of some quality.

BWV 6.1.06; Adnams ***Broadside***, Cheriton ***Pots Ale***, Gale's ***HSB***, Hampshire ***Ironside Best***, Ringwood ***Fortyniner***, ***Old Thumper***, Wychwood ***Hobgoblin***

Platform Tavern

Town Quay, S014 2NY. Telephone 02380 337232
www.platformtavern.com
Gaffer: Stewart Cross
Food: Normal extensive menu plus specials board from sarnies to steaks £3-£10, 12 to 3, 6 to 9 Sat, 12 to 9 Sun. 12 to 8 Roast dinner only
Smoking Throughout
Open: 12 to 11 Mon to Wed. 12 to 11.30 Thu, 12 to 12 Fri and Sat, 12 to 11 Sun

MP TV BM D

The Platform is '*not like your normal comfy but slightly grotty boozer, but more like the smoking room of a rich, eccentric Victorian explorer*.' (integral.soton.ac) My visit was a very pleasant lunchtime, people reading papers in piece and quiet, the staff gearing themselves up for another evening of good music and partying. This is quite a happening place. Bob Ford of Bristol describes it as '*homely, friendly and bohemian. Not a typical football pub but welcoming for fans*.' Peter of Southampton continues saying '*the atmosphere with real footie fans, both home and away is fantastic*.' Near the waterfront bars it offers everything that the modern try to achieve, being something distinctive yet real.
UPDATE: Blues continues to be the pub signature sound although live jazz makes it's way to Sundays. On Sunday the pub will be too busy for a lunchtime visit as Sunday roast is usually fully booked.

BWV 24.8.04: Fullers ***London Pride***, Itchen Valley ***Godfathers***, Wychwood ***Hobgoblin***, Grease ***Lightning***
BWV 6.1.06 Cheriton ***Turkish Delight***, Fullers ***London Pride***, Itchen Valley ***Godfathers***, Timothy Taylor ***Landlord***

Southwestern Arms

38-40 Adelaide Street, St. Denys, SO17 2HW. Telephone 023 80324542
Gaffers: Steve Hoey and Lin Clare
Smoking Throughout
Open: 3.30 to 1 Mon to Thu, 2 to 1 am Fri, 12 to 1 amSat, 12 to 1 am Sun

B

SP TV BM PG

The Good Beer Guide describes this pub as a '*Large, two-storey pub where many corners provide a surprisingly intimate atmosphere*.' Little did I know that when I started this research that this pub, the first I visited would rank so highly among all those I found over the year. A premiership beer house if ever there was one. '*The landlord takes great pride in his constantly-changing range of beers, regularly stocking ten or more. Loads of beers, usually good, usually packed*.' (Wessex Motor club). Steve is indeed fiercely proud of what he has achieved in homely and residential St Denys. This pub was often recommended to my website by those who are willing to get off the train a stop early and chat to locals before the game.
UPDATE: Now more of an emphasis on Wessex regional ales. Festivals likely in July and Nov.

BWV 24.8.04 Badger ***Tanglefoot***, Deuchars ***IPA***, Frog Island ***Shoemaker***, Fullers ***London Pride***, St. Peters ***Best Bitter***, Tanglewood ***Harvest***, Three Rivers ***Summer Rays***, Wychwood ***Hobgoblin***, Ushers ***Summer Madness***
BWV 6.1.06: Caledonian ***Deuchars IPA***, Elgoods ***Snickelmas***, Fullers ***London Pride***, Hopback ***Entire Stout***, ***Summer Lightning***, Ringwood ***Bitter***, Sharp's ***Doombar***, Weymouth ***Jurassic Durdle***, Whitestar ***Crafty Shag***, Weston's ***Old Rosie***, ***Perry***

Southampton

We think it strange that so many people who travel by plane hardly seem bothered about looking out of the window. We love it, and spend a lot of time trying to figure out what we are flying over, because it is difficult to recognise landmarks from a long way up. The only obvious things are football grounds and large bodies of water.

The sea city of Southampton stands in a triangle of land between the river's Itchen and Test, with Southampton Water beyond. With four daily tides this makes for a fine port, but the water made it easy for the Luftwaffe to find, and much was flattened. The rebuilt centre now feels modern and at times strangely empty.

Southampton was a very prosperous mediaeval port, but the merchants did not spend money on building a cathedral sized church, as many other rich towns did then. It has just a modest church to this day. They did not invest in a solid defence either until the after the French had done their usual thing with fire in 1338. A long section of the wall Southampton built after that survives, as does a grand gatehouse and scattered mediaeval buildings.

The *St. Mary's Stadium* is just by the Itchen but it is well worth the half mile walk down to Town Quay Marina. But be warned, if a famous cruise ship is docking or sailing, there will be a bigger crowd than Southampton FC get.

Southend

Years ago, after visiting the ancient wooden church at Greensted, to the north-west of Southend-on-Sea, one of the Bradwan team got stopped by two different Police patrol cars and closely questioned. Both found the idea of someone visiting a church without nicking something only slightly less strange than someone going for a walk in Essex.

Southend Pier

Piers were first built so boats could load at all states of the tide, and ferry traffic was vital to Southend, which is why it ended up with the worlds longest pier stretching over the vast beach and mud flats. The first section was opened in 1889, and the last in 1927. It has suffered damaged many times, and we suspect it was only saved because it is a record holder. It has had a recent cash injection and seemed safe and proud, but then had another fire, which apparently melted the new plastic water mains!

Prittlewell Priory, Priory Park, Victoria Avenue

An ex-Clunic Priory. It has a genuinely rare collection of TVs, wireless and recording equipment made in the EKCO (E K Cole Ltd) factory which used to be just to the north. It is across the road from Roots Hall.

Beecroft Art Gallery, Station Road, Westcliff on Sea

Like all town galleries, that do not have a social climbing director bent on glorifying garbage like Damian Hirst' s hit art, this has pictures you'd like on your own wall; and it has a web gallery so you can view them on-line *www.beecroft-art-gallery.co.uk*

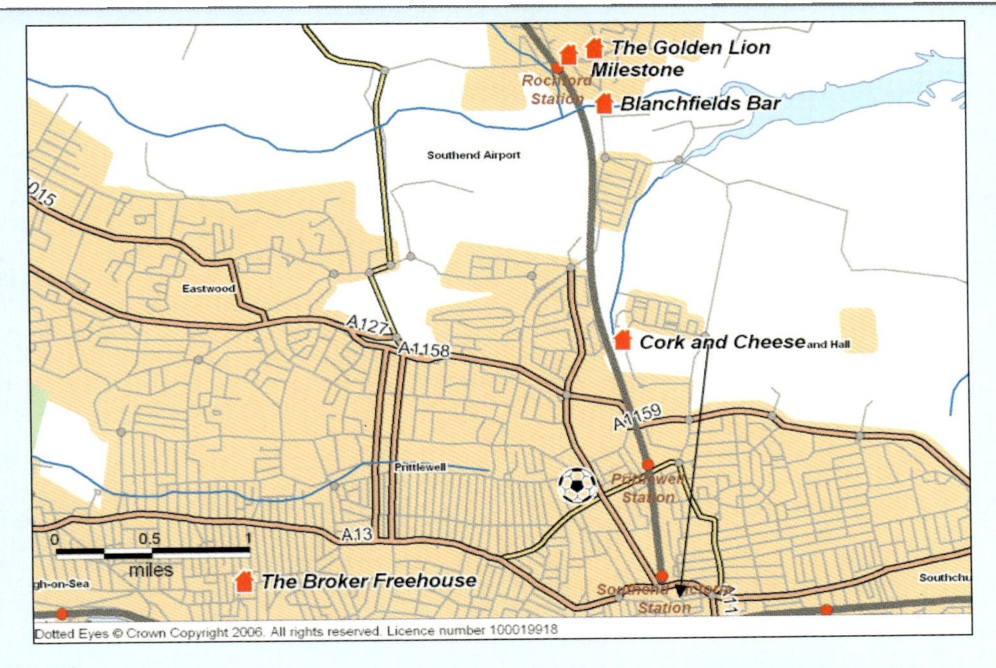

Blanchfields Bar

1 Southend Road, Rochford SS4 1HO. Telephone 01702 544015 New
www.blanchfields.co.uk
Gaffer: Steve Lunn
Food: Good quality all home-made menu using local fresh ingedients and at a good value price 12 to 3, 6 to 9, 12 to 4 Sun (Carvery)
No smoking before 5pm
Open: 11 to 11

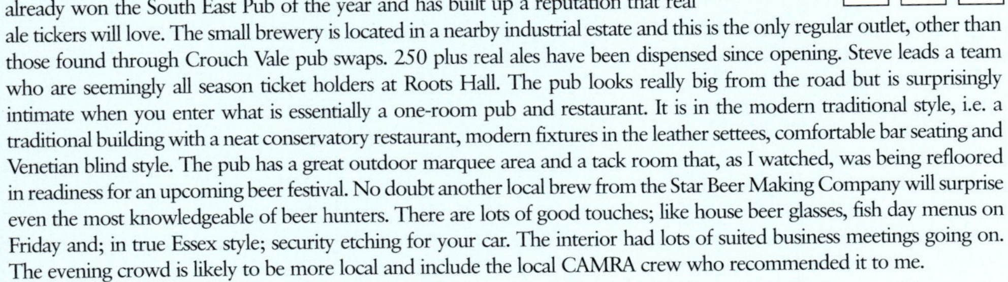

Blanchfields only opened as the Blanchfield brewery tap in August 2005. It has already won the South East Pub of the year and has built up a reputation that real ale tickers will love. The small brewery is located in a nearby industrial estate and this is the only regular outlet, other than those found through Crouch Vale pub swaps. 250 plus real ales have been dispensed since opening. Steve leads a team who are seemingly all season ticket holders at Roots Hall. The pub looks really big from the road but is surprisingly intimate when you enter what is essentially a one-room pub and restaurant. It is in the modern traditional style, i.e. a traditional building with a neat conservatory restaurant, modern fixtures in the leather settees, comfortable bar seating and Venetian blind style. The pub has a great outdoor marquee area and a tack room that, as I watched, was being refloored in readiness for an upcoming beer festival. No doubt another local brew from the Star Beer Making Company will surprise even the most knowledgeable of beer hunters. There are lots of good touches; like house beer glasses, fish day menus on Friday and; in true Essex style; security etching for your car. The interior had lots of suited business meetings going on. The evening crowd is likely to be more local and include the local CAMRA crew who recommended it to me.

BWV 5.4.06: Blanchfield ***IPA Twist***, ***Golden Ball***, Greene King ***IPA***, ***Old Speckled Hen***, Maypole ***Maybee***, Vale ***Best Bitter***, Banham ***Rum Cask Cider***, Snakecatcher ***Cider***, Weston's ***Perry***

The Broker Freehouse

213-217 Leigh Road, Leigh on Sea SS9 1JA. Telephone 01702 471932
Gaffer: Alan and Elaine Gloyne
Food: English cuisine and vegetarian meals plus Sunday lunches
12 to 2.30, 6 to 9 Tue to Sat, 12 to 6 Sun
Separate smoking areas SP SK BM D
Open: 11 to 11

The Broker in question is Alan who left the sugar broking game twelve years ago and has created a great community pub. It gets very busy here at weekends especially if the many footie teams based here are gathered for a game on TV. The pub has plenty of space, being designed with subdivided areas of a large bar. The wow feature comes in the art work that is everywhere in this pub. A photo of the twin towers and a mirror image, apocalyptic, post 9/11 piece by Alan's son stand out in the main bar. There are also numerous other paintings and sketches around the walls often showcasing local artists. And then there is the ale. Regional ales rotate around Spitfire and Young's. This is a top local boozer with a definite touch of class. For me it is a definite choice if travelling by train from Fenchurch Street.
UPDATE: Ignore the train bit, experience shows it is a taxi ride (01702 334455) to the station, Chalkwell is easier. The pub is the only one in the local area to have ten years in the local CAMRA guide and a certificate to prove it. The pub may be refitted in the coming year.

BWV 1.4.05: Adnams ***Bitter***, Fuller's ***London Pride***, Shepherd Neame ***Spitfire***, Young's ***Bitter***
BWV 5.5.06: Everards ***Tiger***, Jennings ***Cumberland Ale***, Shepherd Neame *Spitfire*, Young's ***Bitter***

Cork and Cheese

10 Talza Way, Victoria Plaza, SS2 5BG. Telephone 01702 616914
Gaffer: John Murray
Food: Extensive range of bar snacks and full menu 12 to 2.15 Mon to Fri
Smoking Throughout MP TV JB P
Open: 11 to 11 Mon to Sat. Closed Sun

The Cork and Cheese has been local CAMRA pub of the year for 6 of the last 10 years. My lunchtime visit found it heaving. Locals, office workers, couples and shoppers all found space in the various nooks and crannies in this cleverly designed three-level pub. A later afternoon visit pre-match found it a little quieter. You enter from an unpromising precinct to find a form of real ale heaven. The pub had an air of calm despite the numbers. This is not the home of Chavs, but diamond geezers. The Nethergate came at a cheap price while the others beers added to a list of 2800 beers within the last ten years. Constantly under threat from shopping centre redevelopment, the pub continues to stand alone in the non-existent town centre real ale scene. Parking is found in the centre's multi-storey car park. Access for those with disabilities may be difficult as the pub is a basement bar, but there is an outside seating area.
UPDATE: There are still plans to redevelop the Plaza, apparently beginning in May. The beer policy remains as good as ever and long may it continue.

BWV 1.4.05: Archers ***Around the Maypole***, Bass ***Draught***, Nethergate ***IPA***, Mordue ***Geordie Pride***, Thatcher's ***Cheddar Valley Cider***
BWV 5.5.06: Archers ***Full Time***, Bass ***Draught***, Downton ***Equinox***, Nethergate ***IPA***, Thatcher's ***Cheddar Valley Cider***

The Golden Lion

New

35 North Street, Rochford SS4 1AB Telephone 01702 545487
Gaffer: Sue Williams
Food: By arrangement for groups, phone to check
Smoking Throughout
Open: 11.30 to 11.30

B

SP SKY JB PG

The Golden Lion stands way above the many town centre pubs because it has not only a great traditional building but also a brilliant selection of ever-changing real ales. The pub has long been recognised by the local CAMRA members, no doubt as long as the pub cat, Sammy, has been in residence. Sue has been the boss for the last sixteen years.

The building dates from the 16th century. You will soon notice that the pub has been tastefully extended and the integrity of its timber-framed exterior preserved in a spotless and historic interior. The leaded stained-glass windows with heraldic shields are an interesting topic for fruitless discussion. The regulars sharing the pub on my lunchtime visit were engaged in typical pub and town gossip conversations found in all the best local boozers. The Lion is at the centre of local sporting activity. There are pub footie and cricket teams and a feeling that Sue knows her locals as man and boy and '*good old boy*.' The pub always has a mild among the ever changing guest ales. To describe the décor it is best to imagine the theme of hanging hops and hanging jugs. The walls are all timbered and the atmosphere very reminiscent of the best village locals that alas are fast being lost to modernisation. It is just perfect also for the post-match pint that avoids the crawl into town. It was recommended by Colchester fans passing through by train on their way home and what a great choice it makes.

BWV 5.4.06: Adnams ***Bitter***, Archers ***Crystal Clear***, Crouch Vale ***Blackwater Mild***, ***Brewer's Gold***, Greene King ***Abbot***, Bounds ***Great Western Revival Cider***

Milestone

Union Road, Rochford SS5 1AP. Telephone 01702 544229
Gaffer: Ron Pearce
Smoking Throughout
Open: 10 to 11 Mon to Sat, 12 to 10.30 Sun

Two real ales were perfectly delivered from the barrel on my April Fools day visit. One would be silly not to search out this pub in a town that has several real ale locations. As Tracey said '*this is Rochford's hidden secret*'. The pub is a bit of a curiosity shop. You enter from the beer garden, all seaside murals and patio tables. Then you find a stone-walled farmhouse bar reminiscent of a coastal tavern. The place has real charm yet is a proper local's pub, complete with geezers who will banter for Essex. Ron has a high level rugby pedigree and recent connections; check out the personal photos of the world cup experiences on the wall. It is very handy for the station and local car park. The pub will have plenty of Southend fans who are very friendly and willing to share their love of real ale. The beers on offer increase to four, nothing from hand pull. As for their recommendations, it isn't '*as good as the Pork n' pie in town*' though, I never did find it, funny that! *UPDATE*: The weekend guest is likely to be from Mighty Oak and, true to their tradition, cooled by jacket.

BWV 1.4.05: Greene King ***IPA***, ***Tanners Jack***
BWV 5.4.06: Greene King ***IPA***

FOOTBALL AND REAL ALE GUIDE

DIVISION ONE PUB OF THE YEAR

As voted for by the readers 2006-07

The Fighting Cock

21-23 Preston Street, Bradford

BWV 14.3.05: Bank Top *Port O'Call*, Glentworth *Early Spring*, Greene King *Abbot*, Holden's *Thigh Bones*, Kelburn *Goldihops*, Old Mill *Bitter*, Phoenix *White Monk*, Theakston's *Old Peculier*, Timothy Taylor *Golden Best*, *Landlord*, Biddenden's *Dry Cider*, Monk's Delight *Cider*, Weston's *Old Rosie*

BWV.1.3.06: Bradfield *Blonde*, Castle Rock *Hemlock*, Copper Dragon *Golden Pippin*, Goose Eye, *Golden Eye*, Greene King *Abbot*, Old Mill *Bitter*, Phoenix *White Monk*, Pictish *Brewers Gold*, Theakston's *Old Peculier*, Timothy Taylor *Best*, *Golden Best*, *Landlord*, Biddenden *Dry*, Monk's Delight *Cider*, Weston's *Old Rosie*

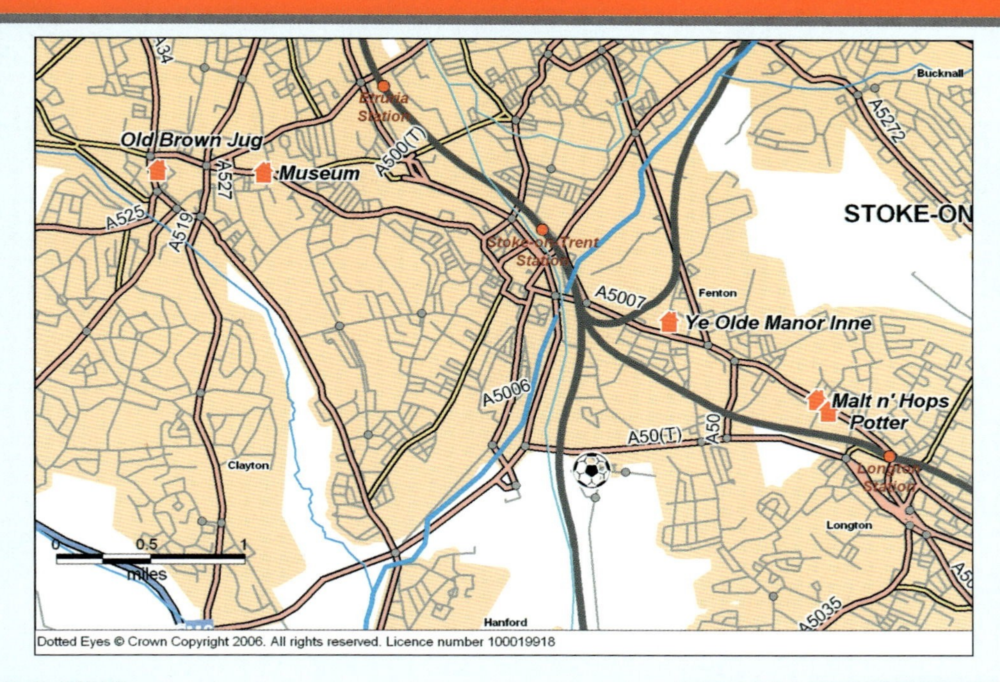

Malt N' Hops

295 King Street, ST4 3EJ. Telephone 01782 313406
Gaffer: Scott Turner
Food: Sandwiches from 12
Smoking Throughout
Open: 12 to 4, 7 to 11.

The bar slogan below the bar says *'If you want to stay longer, come early.'* This is good advice for this simple, honest, street boozer that offers beers from the Tower stable under their own house label. This is the closest decent pub to the Britannia but not on the obvious trail over the myriad of sky walks. Amidst the ever-declining factory workshops *'this pub gives glimpses of the reality of Potteries life.'* My visit found the locals in the smaller TV bar, ready for the horse-racing and beer session. The range of forthcoming beers on the chalk board showed that there is a real demand for quality alternatives to national chain ales. To complement this list are masses of rarer bottled ales and the option of hand-pull or from the wood. It will be busy on matchdays, yet has ample room as the rear lounge offers extra room, and the welcome is guaranteed to be good. This is a damn good boozer. *UPDATE*: An impressive list of European beers is added to by the 7 or 8 ever-changing guest ales.

BWV 10.3.05: Archers ***Special***, Beowulf ***Mercian Slave***, Greene King ***Abbot***, Malt n' Hops ***Dark, Bursley Bitter***, ***Mild***, Tower ***Tower of Strength***, Weetwood ***Ambush***
BWV 2.11.05: Acorn ***Barnsley Gold***, Caledonian ***Edinburgh Strong Ale***, Cottage ***GWR***, Fuller's ***ESB***, Greene King ***Ab***bot, Malt n' Hops ***Bursley Bitter***, ***Dark Mild***

Museum

24 George Street, Newcastle Under Lyme, ST5 1JU. Telephone 01782 623866
Gaffer: Paul Blackburn
Food: Light snacks from 12
Smoking Throughout
Open: 12 to 11 Mon to Sat, 12 to 10.30 Sun.

I instantly fell for the simple charms of this must-not-miss pub in the Potteries. The place was busy, early evening with groups of regulars that made it somewhere to remember. The professionals in their suits congregated in the right hand bar, the educated artisans found their regular spaces in the cosy and comfortable public bar. This pub has an obvious self-regulating nature brought about by the love of considered conversation and quality ale. Judging by the conversation regarding their footie teams, the punters are not always locals. This is a hostelry for cigars as well as ciggies, for beer rather than brawn, for conversation not idle chat. It is a great pub, no doubt. On my visit the footie match on the TV was almost incidental to the serious supping. Once the game was over little changed, apart that the beer choices kept changing as others punters arrived to get settled into what appeared to be a regular and easy-going real ale fest.
UPDATE The Museum is lovingly still the same. The Museum Brew is from Tower!

BWV 10.3.05: Bass ***Draught***, Elgood's ***Old Wagg***, Holden's ***Thigh Bones***, Worthington's ***Bitter***, Biddenden's ***Cider***
BWV 2.12.05: Holden's ***Golden Glow***, Museum Brewing Co. ***Joules Bitter***, Shepherd Neame ***Spitfire***, Worthington's ***Bitter***

Old Brown Jug

41 Bridge Street, ST5 2RY, Telephone 07751 964815
www.thebrownjug.co.uk
Gaffers: Nigel and Louise Woolliscroft
Food: Home-cooked, freshly prepared English cuisine from 12
Smoking Throughout with extractor fans
Open: 6 to 11/12 Mon to Thu, 12 to 1am Fri. and Sat, 12 to 12.30am Sun

This pub is a pleasant surprise. *'The joint oozes sophistication of the sweaty kind through a positive love of Jazz and Blues.'* The relaxed nature is evident throughout the day as the ambience is one of reserved charm which gives way to cool as the music gets to take pride of place. Check out the great photos and the blues family tree near the bar. Or alternatively, chill out to the guest ales that add to regular Marston's picks. My visit found serial cross-worders enjoying an early evening chat while other young lovers arrived at the obvious meeting point in town. The locals also rave about the events of summer *'when barbecue and impromptu outdoor jamming are known to break out of the bar into the garden.'* In the evening the more romantic are catered for by lowering the lighting and letting candlelight go to work.
UPDATE: The brightest, biggest and best beer garden in the town is a major new feature. A jazz club on Tuesdays continues the live music tradition. Blues is centre-stage on Sundays.

BWV 10.3.05: Brains ***Rev James***, Marston's ***Pedigree***, ***Old Empire***, Weston's ***Old Rosie Cider***, Bounds ***Brand Cider***
BWV 2.12.05: Jennings ***Cocker Hoop***, ***Cumberland Ale***, ***Sneckliftter***, Marston's ***Owd Roger***, ***Pedigree***, Weston's ***Scrumpy***

Potter

432 King Street, ST4 3DB. Telephone 01782 311968
Gaffer: Nigel Hurst
Smoking Throughout
Open: 12 to 11, Mon to Fri, 11 to 11 Sat, 12 to 10.30 Sun

SP SKY BM PG

This is a small, main-road pub that has a real quality and class that belies its location. *'It is a very popular pub among locals and travelling ale-hunters alike.'* I arrived too early for their Spring beer festival but it is evident from the beers on offer that the pub is one where one can find some alternatives to the usual Staffordshire choices. The pub gets crowded when it screens footie on the box. I would choose a less busy time when the chat is of real issues, mulled over quality ale. The rear bar is taken up with a pool table, the front bar needs no diversion from serious supping. The entire pub has a light and airy feel, wooden floors and plaster walls giving it a lived-in but well-loved appeal. The Coach House ale as a regular was something of a pleasant surprise, but then again the Potteries were proving to have many such challenges to my prejudiced pre-conceptions.
UPDATE The recommendation of Gillingham fans is that this is as good as ever for a pre-match, but not necessarily a post-match pint. Nothing wrong with the pub, but the police will make it difficult to return. London Pride will be the regular ale when you visit.

BWV 10.3.05: Coach House ***Dick Turpin***, Downton ***Chimera Red***, Fuller's ***ESB***, Goff's ***Launcelot***, Greene King ***Abbot***, Robinson's ***Unicorn***
BWV 2.12.05: Coach House ***Dick Turpin***, Fuller's ***ESB***, Greene King ***Abbot***, Lancaster ***Good Will***, Wells ***Christmas Cracker***, Weston's ***Old Rosie Cider***

Ye Olde Manor Inne

Manor Street, Fenton, ST4 2PT. Telephone 01782 763693 New
Gaffer: Sam Yewdell
Food: Homemade food with restaurant and Sunday lunches
11 to 3, 5 to 7 Mon to Sat, 12 to 3 Sun
Separate smoking areas
Open: 11 to 12

The Manor was recommended by Nigel and Scott, and it proved to be an excellent choice. Sam rescued and re-opened the pub in 1999 and has created a comfortable farmhouse-style pub that has a really cosy feel. The two regular ales are complemented by two weekly-changing guests and the locals rated the quality highly. Phil, one of a lunch time group of pub lunchers, went further to say *'the staff are helpful and they are gorgeous'*. They were not talking about Sam here! The pub looks large from the outside but is creatively sub-divided into five separate areas all off a central bar.

The pub had a really friendly atmosphere when I visited. It will be pretty busy on matchdays but more so on the weekend evenings when entertainment draws people from an area larger than the regulars' local distance. Those locals appear to like their pubs dimly lit, but the effect was to emphasise the fire that stands at one end of the bar and reinforce the cosy atmosphere. As with all Stoke pubs, it is a good walk to the ground. This one is, however, a good and simple walk from the main station, away from the town centre. I really liked the conversation that, on my visit, had such a family focus, i.e. the merits of the latest play station and how to help sponsor the latest school activity. This would be my choice if I wanted to avoid football grub and perhaps, if I was with friends, who wanted quality, well-known ales

BWV 2.12.05: Bass *Draught*, Fuller's *Discovery*, Wells *Bombardier*, Worthington *Draught*

Stoke

Stoke-on-Trent must be the strangest city in the country. It is made up of six towns forced together by Government pressure and common sense in 1888against fierce 'local patriotism'. They all had coal but grew on clay, which some potters dug out of the King's highway in the days of mud tracks; but because no one town was greatly richer than the rest, and because pot making did not need tall mills with taller chimneys, there are no massive buildings and no real centre.

Stoke was not even the biggest town, but probably named the city because it had the parish church, so the other 5 are now only known to people that live there; and quiz nutters. The church is probably the only thing in Stoke town worth seeing. It has lots of monuments to the pottery owning rich who have returned to the clay, which they obviously hoped would be remolded rather than fired at high temperatures.

Of the other towns Hanley is the largest, the main shopping centre, and the site of both the Museum and Art Gallery, and the Etruria Industrial Museum (which is set in a bone and flint grinding mill that worked until 1972); Burslem is the oldest town (see Port Vale); and Longton has the Gladstone Pottery Museum. This leaves you needing to remember Tunstall and Fenton to get your quiz point.

Oat cakes

This seems to be the ethnic cuisine of Stoke, and comes highly recommend, especially if served with bacon.
www.stoke.gov.uk

Sunderland

Sunderland has always had two geographical challenges. The first is that nobody ever goes through Sunderland. It is by the sea, and while Sunderland has always been a port it never benefited from large volumes of general trade or passengers. It grew on exporting coal and, according to the Port's website, is now a 'modern short-sea specialist, which has a growing portfolio of customers, recognition of our ability to compete with our bigger neighbours'
Competing with bigger neighbours, or rather neighbour, is Sunderland's other challenge. No other big English city, expect possibly Bradford, seems so overshadowed by a not much bigger neighbour. It was sucked into Tyne and Wear, there are no direct trains to London, and the many Mackem builders we have met were called Geordie by their mates.

Sunderland Council website is straightforward but has no tourist page. There is tourist stuff, but finding the exchange rate for the Mongolian Tugrik online would be easier.
There is a good ***Winter Gardens***. The attached museum had 150,000 visitors a year, but shut in 1999. It will be reopened; some time this side of the Sahara blooming and Sunderland sharing ***St. James Park***, but will be based on visitor consultation so is likely to be something that no individual bureaucrat will take the blame for. There is also the ***National Glass Centre***, but the website is gushing and says too much about what it is dedicated to and hardly anything about what is on permanent display, if anything.

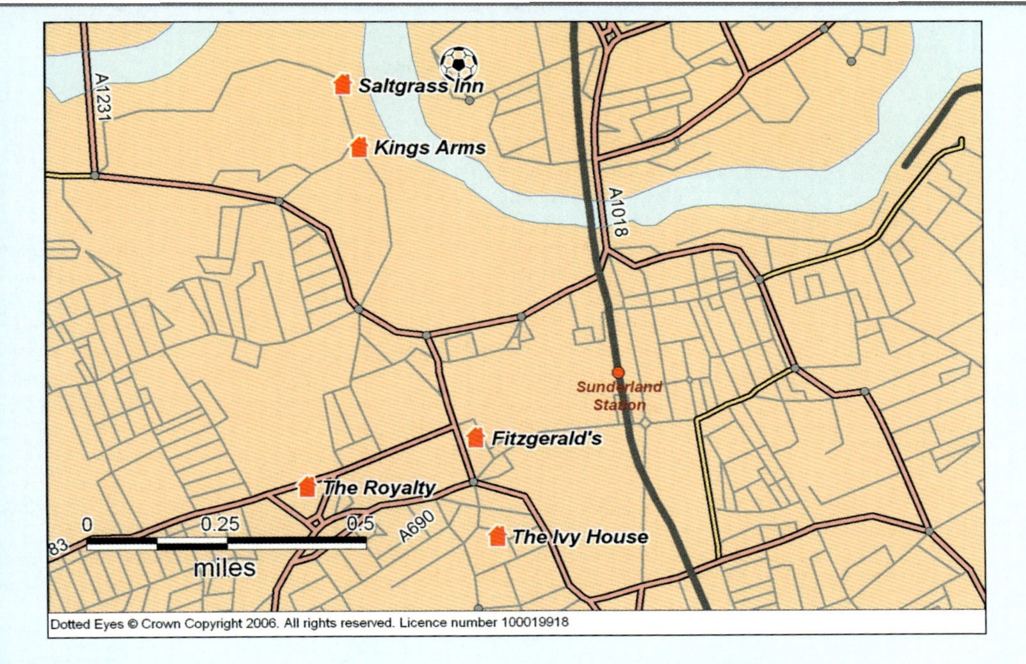

Fitzgerald's

10-12 Green Terrace, SR1 3PZ Telephone 0191 567 0852
www.fitzgeralds.co.uk
Gaffer: Matt Alldis
Food: Varied menu to suit all tastes 11 to 3, 12 to 3 Sun
Separate smoking areas
Open: 11 to 11, 12 to 11 Sun

Ten constantly-changing beers are found here in an area popular with both young and old. This pub changes as the different groups come and go. It is sometimes very crowded, yet at other times it offers real tranquillity. There is always a quality selection of real ales, particularly northern ales. It is quite a large pub, offering separate sections rather than rooms. Apparently the wireless internet access is proving popular with business trade and regulars alike.

I enjoyed sitting in the rear of the pub chatting with a couple of old-timers who were keen to stress the friendliness of the staff as a major factor in it being their choice. They were also keen to make sure they had a seat before the younger crowd came in for their usual beer and chat-up session.

UPDATE: Fitzgerald's continues to offer great ale, and the beer garden is likely to be improved.

BWV 13.1.05: Archers ***Pixie Juice***, ***Scatty Cow***, Brains ***SA***, Cains ***Raisin***, Greene King ***Morland Original***, Harviestoun ***Jack the Lad***, Orkney ***Skull Splitter***, Thwaites ***Original***, Ushers ***Winter Storm***, Weston's ***Country Perry***

BWV 10.2.06: 3 Rivers ***IPA***, ***GMT***, Archers ***Best***, Boggart Hole Clough ***Bog Eyed***, Dark Star ***Espresso Stout***, ***Hophead***, Empire ***Long Bow***, Isle of Mull ***Island Pale Ale***, Wharfedale ***Folly Gold***, Weston's ***Country Perry***

B

CP SKY BM D

Kings Arms

1 Hanover Place, SR4 6BU. Telephone 0191 567 8094
www.thekingsarms.org
Gaffer: Lucie Young
Food: Toasted sandwiches
Smoking Throughout
Open: 11.30 to 11, 11.30 to 12 Fri and Sat

This is a place to find rare micro-brews '*that are tip top and blows your doors in.*' (Steve Potts) The Guvn'or is a relentless hunter of real ale and the customers come from afar to sample. My visit was one of my highlights of the year's research, thanks to the easy conversation and genuine warmth of the bar-flies. As Jean Downey says '*It's great because of the pre-match banter between friends and strangers alike.*' Mickie Downey goes on to say that '*it has a great pre-match atmosphere, full of football families of all ages and friendly away fans.*' They will, however, spin some tales of fans getting a boat to the game. Better to walk via the river-side path or get a taxi. It has '*good beer, good, craic, live football and I go.*' (Kipper) It can't have everything I suppose.
UPDATE: Local CAMRA Pub of the Year 2005, iPod music is available; an outdoor marquee is in place.

BWV 13.1.05: Anglo Dutch ***Spike's on T'Way***, Concertina ***One Eyed Jack***, Glentworth ***White***, Ossett ***Silver King***, Wentworth ***Bumble Bee***
BWV 10.2.06: Abbeydale ***Matins***, Castle Rock ***Harvest Pale***, Halifax ***Joker***, Harviestoun ***Bitter and Twisted***, Newby Wyke ***Grantham Gold***, Northumberland ***Bucking Fastard***, Oakham ***JHB***, Timothy Taylor ***Landlord***, Saxon ***Diamond Lil Cider***

CP SKY JB PG D

The Ivy House

New

Worcester Terrace, SR2 7AY. Telephone 0191 567 3399
Gaffer: Bob Fairlie
Food: Good quality student-style food 11 to 2, not Sun
Smoking Throughout
Open: 11 to 11, 12 to 10.30 Sun

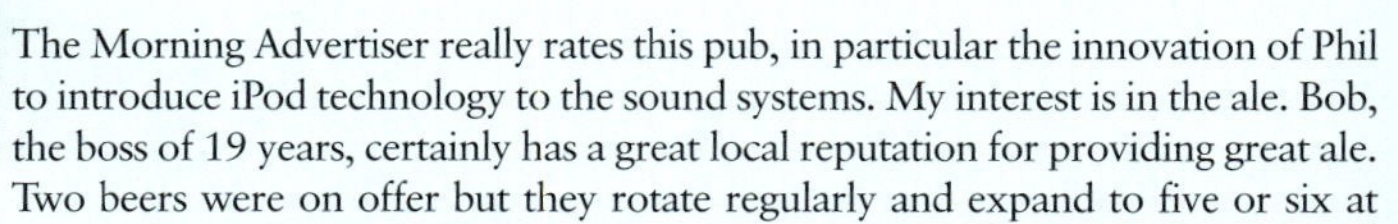

The Morning Advertiser really rates this pub, in particular the innovation of Phil to introduce iPod technology to the sound systems. My interest is in the ale. Bob, the boss of 19 years, certainly has a great local reputation for providing great ale. Two beers were on offer but they rotate regularly and expand to five or six at weekends. This is when the pub gets very busy. The students give way to town regulars seeking something out of the central shopping drag. The Ivy House is surprisingly convenient for a back-street pub. It is just up the road from the local bus station and between two metro stations, no more than five minutes away.

Of interest to pub architects is the hemispherical design caused by the pub being a 1950s conversion of three separate houses. Owned now by Barracuda, the push is on to offer real ale in their houses. The Ivy sets a good example of how it will appeal to a very wide range of customers. Bob was insistent that the eclectic tastes of his customers mean the place is rarely routine or even predictable. This sounded just perfect for a visitor. It is very friendly and lively. The pool table was ignored by Ray, who obviously didn't want to be thrashed again. '*You know you will love it*' says the bar top slogan. I am sure this is true.

BWV 9.2.06: Black Sheep ***Bitter,*** Darwin ***Ivy***, ***Evolution***

The Royalty

New

88 Chester Road, SR2 7PR. Telephone 0191 565 9930
Gaffer: Paul Ward
Food: Menu geared for students, i.e. hearty and good value 11 to 7, 12 to 6 Sun
Smoking Throughout
Open: 11 to 11, 12 to 10.30 Sun

CP SKY JB PG D

Real ale came to the Royalty in the summer of 2005 and the pub had reached the point, by the time of my February visit, that two ales were being proposed, as each guest (and there are only guest ales), were changing every two days. Paul and Ben, the assistant manager, were very keen to continue the trend, recognising the link between the University customers and their love of ale. The links with academia go further when you chat with Ben and find out about the brewing research that goes on just down the road.

The pub is very large and advertises a no baseball caps or track-suit policy. On matchdays the range of students means that almost any shirt might be found. The pub is very convenient for the sign-posted matchday parking. The student-priced food will also satisfy many a fan. The pub is lively yet friendly, large yet comfortable. The end of the pub we chose had a pool table, the central area is flag-stoned, the other end separated into a carpeted lounge. It is significantly the home of the Sunderland surfing crowd. The TV was tuned to the tide table pages on Ceefax and, as the wind increased, I witnessed an event that was new to me. Phone calls were made and locals found excuses to head for the coast. I really liked the atmosphere in the Royalty. It deserves to do well, if only for the future of real ale, as these locals graduate and take their enthusiasm with them into future careers elsewhere.

BWV 9.2.06: Tetley's ***Cask Bitter***

Saltgrass Inn

37 Hanover Place, Deptford, SR4 6BY. Telephone 0191 565 7229
www.thesaltgrass.com
Gaffer: Daryl Frankland
Food: Bar food/snacks, plus home-cooked, freshly-prepared, restaurant menu 12 to 3, 5 to 10
Separate smoking areas
Open: 11 to 11, 11 to 12 Fri and Sat, 12 to 11 Sun

SP BM

Do you remember seaside, scrimshaw and seashell pubs? Well in Deptford, among the riverside warehouses, you can find the Saltgrass. It is dark and comfortable, intimate and cosy, a place to revel in winter warmth. The banter alone is well worth the taxi ride. Andrew of Houghton praises the '*great pre-match atmosphere*.' Similarly John Watson of York says '*what more could you want than well-kept beers with friendly staff and regulars, and a good real fire?*' While '*the fire keeps some in on freezing days when the lads are playing below par*', for Dave '*it is the barmaids, who are dead fit*'. Daryl is one of those landlords who sell their businesses as their passion. Any real ale fan will learn masses from spending time in his company. The guest ale choice is always reliably good, mixing well-known brands with rarer regional ales. *UPDATE*: The planned Wearside regeneration is the hot topic, and can only be good news.

BWV 13.1.05: Bass ***Draught***, Black Sheep ***Bitter***, Caledonian ***Deuchars IPA***, Weston's ***Scrumpy***
BWV 10.2.06: Black Sheep ***Bitter***, Caledonian ***Deuchars IPA***, Everard's ***Tiger***, Wychwood ***Hobgoblin***

FOOTBALL AND REAL ALE GUIDE

DIVISION TWO PUB OF THE YEAR

As voted for by the readers 2006-07

Birkbeck Tavern

45 Langthorne Road, Leytonstone

BWV 25.1.05: Barnsley *Oakwell Bitter*, Rita's Special (*House Brew*), St. Austell *Tinners*, Skinner's *Betty Stogs*

BWV 12.4.06: Archers *Spring Blonde*, Rita's Special (*House Brew*), Welton's *Old Cocky*, *Randy Rabbit*

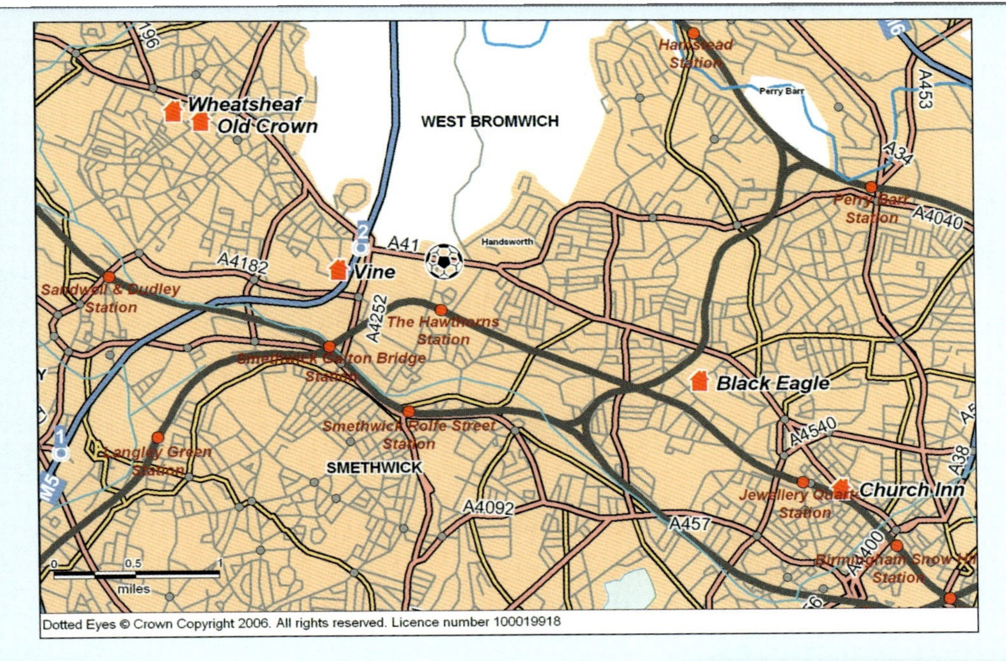

Black Eagle

New

16 Factory Road, Hockley, B18 5JU. Telephone 0121 523 4008
Gaffer: Tony Lewis
Food: Excellent home-cooked traditional English fayre 12 to 2.30, 5.30 to 9.30 (Bar), 7.30 to 9.30 (Restaurant). No food Sun evening
Restaurant non-smoking
Open: 11.30 to 3, 5.30 to 11 Mon to Thu, 11 to 11 Fri, 12 to 3, 7 to 11 Sat, 12 to 3 only Sun

B

SP BM D

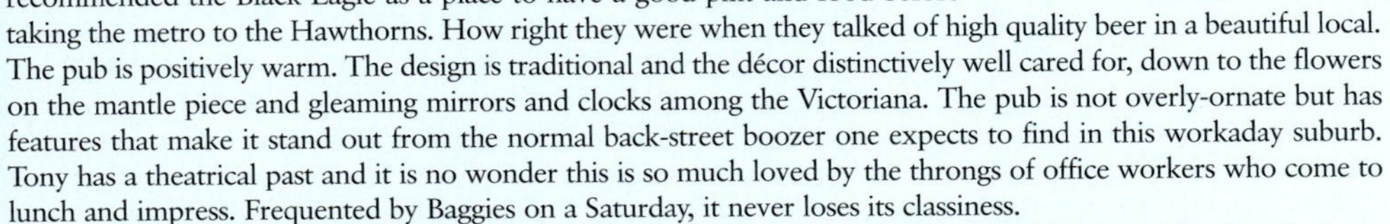

Geoff Clarke and the London branch of the Baggies supporters club recommended the Black Eagle as a place to have a good pint and food before taking the metro to the Hawthorns. How right they were when they talked of high quality beer in a beautiful local. The pub is positively warm. The design is traditional and the décor distinctively well cared for, down to the flowers on the mantle piece and gleaming mirrors and clocks among the Victoriana. The pub is not overly-ornate but has features that make it stand out from the normal back-street boozer one expects to find in this workaday suburb. Tony has a theatrical past and it is no wonder this is so much loved by the throngs of office workers who come to lunch and impress. Frequented by Baggies on a Saturday, it never loses its classiness.

I had a very pleasant lunchtime sat in the sun-lit front bar. The tone is set by Radio 2 which subtly invites a reflective and peaceful attitude to drinking here. It meets the needs of foodies, drinkers and couples merely chatting, equally well. It is recommended to book for food in the rear restaurant-lounge. I would be perfectly content to hog a corner in one of the two bars for a long session.

BWV 18. 11 .05: Ansells ***Bitter***, ***Mild***, Batham ***Best Bitter***, Burton Bridge ***Stairway to Heaven***, Hadrian and Border ***Reiver's IPA***, Marston's ***Pedigree***, Timothy Taylor ***Landlord***

The Church Inn

22 Great Hampton Street, Hockley, B18 6AQ. Telephone 0121 515 1851
Gaffer: Ray Wilkes
Food: Good, honest, traditional pub food, with large helpings 12 to 2, 6 to 9
Smoking Throughout
Open: 11 to 11 Mon to Thu, 11 to 3, 6 to 11 Sat, closed all day Sun

The Church Inn is a fantastic boozer in a rather neglected part of rapidly-regenerating Birmingham. What it lacks in location it makes up for in massive meals of high quality and a no-nonsense attitude to good ales. As local lad Ian said *'You have got to come here, it's pucka! The food is awesome and the company just great'* In a change to the normal pattern, it is the evening that brings out the professionals, using the pub as somewhere very different to the traditional town haunt. On matchdays the pub is heaving, whoever is playing in town. I enter it in the Baggies page but it could equally be a base before visiting Villa or the Blues.

The pub has three bars, the most interesting being the secluded back bar, a bit of a secret den for those who like a bit of privacy! I guess the *'£28 Honey Monster grill'* is really for 7 people to share, rather than the challenge of get it free if you do the impossible and eat it within a single session. It rightly proclaims itself as a heritage inn; the design is quirkily charming, down to the gingham table cloths that dress every table. Carol behind the bar is a bit of a real ale fans' legend. She alone was identified by others as a reason to go to the pub. Others talked of the legendary whisky selection. For me it was a long-lasting pint and a short trip to the local metro station before the hop back home from Snow Hill.

BWV 19.11.05: Batham ***Best Bitter***, Greene King ***IPA***

Old Crown

56 Sandwell Road, B70 8TG. Telephone 0121 525 4600
Gaffers: Pat and Julie Patel
Food: Full menu most of the week, reduced on match-days but Indian snacks and rolls available, 12 to 4, 6 to 9 (not Mon eve.)
Two non-smoking areas, good ventilation and cleaners
Open: 12 to 4, 5 to 11, 7.30 to 10.30 Sun

This pub is a throw-back to how I imagine pubs were in the 70s. Retaining traditional values in the seating, décor and quality of service, this is a truly friendly side-street local. The pub is not only for Baggies friendships, *'we have Blues, Villa, Wolves and Walsall and the rapport is fantastic,'* (Geoff Clarke of Wednesbury) Pat and the customers *'welcome good beer, good food and good humour from all who call in, whatever their team.'* (David Davies), You can see the obvious family ties with the food ethos found at the Vine, (As Ron of West Bromwich says, it has *'a good friendly atmosphere for home and away supporters to toast a good result with award winning ales.'* The Midland Pub Co and Evening Star plaudits are well deserved: as they say, this is *'the perfect pub.'*
UPDATE: Good news! Pat is back home after some time in hospital, and the pub continues to serve great real ale.

BWV 22.2.05: Archers ***Golden Ale***, Malvern Hills ***Dr. Gully's Winter Ale***, Old Crown (Ma Pardoe's) ***Entire***, Wessex ***Kilmington Best***, Thatcher's ***Cider***
BWV 18.11.05: Bath Ales ***Best***, Greene King ***Abbot***, Jennings ***Red Breast***, ***Snecklifter***

The Vine

152 Roebuck Street, B70 6RD. Telephone 0121 553 2866
www.sukis.co.uk
Gaffer: Suki Patel
Food: Tandoori barbecue and speciality curries and baltis, pub grub
11.30 to 2.30, 5 to 11 Mon to Thu, 12 to 11 Fri and Sat, 12 to 10.30 Sun
Separate smoking areas
Open: 11.30 to 2.30, 5 to 11 Mon to Thu, 11.30 to 11 Fri,
12 to 11 Sat and Sun

On my many visits to this ground-breaking pub, the atmosphere has always been the same. Crowded and lively, it has a '*great atmosphere, friendly staff, good real ale selection*' (Adam of C Heath). It has been extended, extended and extended again so that the original bar is tiny compared to the series of canteen style dining spaces that stretch, it seems, back as far as the nearby M5. Mark says '*that if you can be happy after watching the Baggies there must be something in the beer.*' The single real ale is always changing so the choice is as surprising as the food is cheap and good. '*Away supporters are welcomed*' (Chris Whitehouse) and '*where else would you find so many footie experts.*' (Rose of Sedgeley). Suki makes a great effort to make the casual visitor as welcome as the regular Baggies who swamp this pub on matchdays. Get there early if you want a seat.
UPDATE: Still no food over a fiver and Batham's will soon be back as the house ale.

BWV 22.2.05: Batham ***Best Bitter***
BWV 18.11.05: Burton Bridge ***Bindle Stiff***

Wheatsheaf

379 High Street, B70 3QW. Telephone 0121 553 4221
Gaffer: Dave Forrest
Food: Good traditional pub-food including Black Country specialties and
Sunday lunch 12 to 3
Smoking Throughout
Open: 11 to 11

SP SKY BM D

The Wheatsheaf is located '*between the doctor's surgery and the church, handy for Baggies fans.*' (Dawn of West Bromwich) The Holden's beer is the major attraction, especially as Dave serves a good range that suits most tastes, and it was very good. The pub has been extended to the rear and the lounge has a stately-home feel. I preferred the smaller front bar, like a market-town tap room and the best bet for chat with the locals and footie fans.

On non-matchdays take a paper and do, as the regulars do, relax, chill out and drink Holden's by numbers. For example Mike Stevens of Dudley waxes, '*before the Baggies game I get a golden body that's wet, goes down with a fantastic head – Holden's Black Country Bitter, beautiful.*' Oo er missus! I'll have some of what he's on. Jimmy of Dudley says '*the match-day special is bostin*!' It is a very good real ale pub.
UPDATE: Dawn's alias has been blown and the pub has Tom Watsons' (Local MP) recommendation for top quality ales.

BWV 22.2.05: Holden's ***Black Country Bitter, Golden Glow, Passionate Monk, Special***
BWV 18.11.05: Holden's ***Black Country Bitter, Black Country Mild, Golden Glow, Horn Dance, Special***

West Bromwich

The Hawthorns is WBA's fifth ground. It was built, in 1900; on land once owned by Sandwell Park Colliery in what was an empty industrial no man's land a mile south of West Bromwich, but only a penny tram ride from the Birmingham suburbs of Handsworth and Smethwick. Now a days so many league football clubs have moved to brown field sites to secure the future of club directors that fans are used to trekking to the middle of nowhere, but 20 years ago the Hawthorns was about the only ground surrounded by almost nothing.

Birmingham has a new tram system, which passes the Hawthorns. It runs paralleled to a railway line and shares stations, but train and tram platforms were separated by a fence, you could not use a ticket for one on the other, and there were no sign in the stations to tell you there is even a choice, let alone any help in making one; and it doesn't even go near New Street, which makes it pointless as a mass transit system.

Oak House Museum

A half timbered Tudor house not far from the Hawthorns, it used to be full of stuffed animals and dead butterflies but now has loan exhibits from the Victoria and Albert Museum. It does Tudor 're-enactments'. So that will be some members of Equity dressing up and off the dole for a few months. www.birminghamuk.com/oakhouse

Wolverhampton

King Aethelred the Unready gave this place to Lady Wulfrana in 985, and the inhabitants are called Wulfranians, although we are not sure who by. The rest of the West Midlands undoubtedly call them something a lot easier to pronounce. This is the kind of town that people assume is grim, probably because most visitors only come to see the football, and few football grounds are in the pretty part of town. There are no flash attractions to draw the slack jawed into the centre, so most pass it by.

St Peter's Church

A big, impressive red church with some good carvings. If it had been made a cathedral Wolverhampton would have become a cultural centre, and making it one would have made geographical, architectural and ecclesiastical sense, but the Church of England follows a higher calling, namely almighty tradition: and English tradition is firmly rooted in the virtues of bumbling and denial; as football fans will know.

Wolverhampton Art Gallery

This has some 'Pop' Art,' note the capital letters. Proper noun status is awarded to a ragbag set of 'artists' by modern art bureaucrats to make the art books they write easier to sell. The pop art here does not include any paintings of Slade, or by Noddy Holder. They done have some nice old paintings that they are a bit ashamed of.

Food

There are good pie shops in the centre of town, including one that sells hot pork sandwiches with apple sauce, and crackling. Emmmmm crackling!

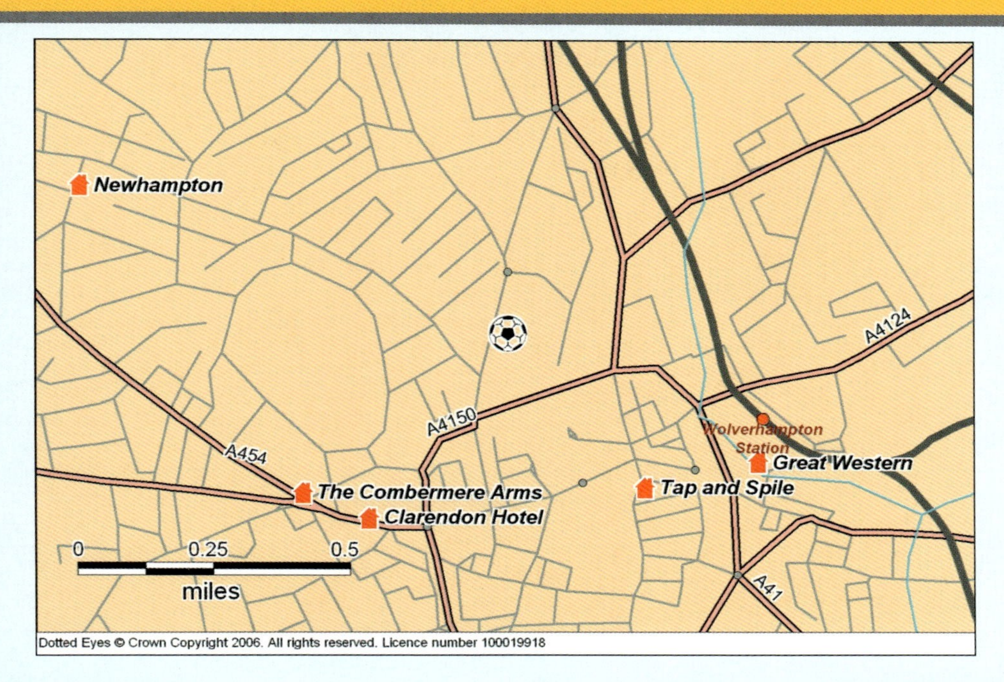

Clarendon Hotel

38 Chapel Ash, WV3 0TN. Telephone 01902 420587
Gaffers: Ray and Angela Payne
Food: Wide ranging menu to suit all needs plus sandwich/beefburger bar on Wolves matchdays. 12 to 3, 5 to 9, Mon to Fri, 12 to 6 Sat
Separate smoking areas
Open: 10 to 11 Mon to Sat

This hotel is something different to my normal style of pub. The Clarendon is geared up for the younger real ale drinker. It has a big pub style and attitude to match yet is very welcoming in contrast to its town centre look-alikes. There is a TV in view of every seat in the pub. On matchdays the baguette bar goes into footie food mode. In the shadow of the Wolverhampton and Dudley Brewery the pub acts as the Banks's tap room and as expected, the beer on my visit was superb. You will need to get in early on matchdays, why not? – it makes sense to get a bit of Banks's when you come to the West Midlands. This is ideal for watching the lunchtime premiership game before strolling across the park to the ground. If only all Wolves fans would understand that for some it makes a perfect day, the stroll, that is.

UPDATE: Ron has moved on and Ray and Angela were at the helm on my visit. They aim to use the pub facilities to the full, i.e. using the function rooms upstairs and continuing to serve top quality ale. The pub does not do accommodation despite the name.

BWV 21.2.05: Banks's *Bitter*, *Original*
BWV 11.11.05: Banks's *Bitter*, *Original*

The Combermere Arms

New

90 Chapel Ash, WV3 0TY. Telephone 01902 421880
Gaffer: Gavin Craig
Food: Award Winning (Midlands sandwich pub of the year, runner up) light lunches
Separate smoking areas
Open: 11 to 3, 5.30 to 11 Mon to Fri, 11 to 11 Sat and Sun

How did I fail to find this last year? Perhaps the Ley lines of Chapel Ash were taking me into some sort of parallel universe. The Chapel Ash Freehouse has recently changed to a Punch house but the philosophy of quality real ale in a cracking and beautiful pub will live on under Gavin's' leadership. Three totally separate rooms plus a rather distinctive courtyard are so characterful that they are defined in folklore by the groups who frequent them The Wolves fans congregate before and after home games in the *'Room of Doom*,' their numbers being swollen in some years by the now famous Swedish Wolves. They always want to conduct a post-match analysis along the lines of '*we were lucky to lose*' Gavin is the king of the quote, a sound bite sensation, and so my hour on a wet Friday gave me a small taste of the humour that is also found. A tree in the toilets? True, and there is so much more. Reading fans also make a major detour, using this on a trip to Cardiff! Perhaps this is because the welcome is so distinctively friendly.

Students and professionals make up the locals clientele often in the "shady place for shady people." Real ale drinking makes up 60% or more of the pub business. The front bar is non smoking. The pub is also a regular haunt for local CAMRA members. The beer list may well return to the extended list that included rarer guest ales. The locals apparently have a particular palate for Enville brews.

BWV 11.11.05: Banks's ***Bitter***, ***Mild***, Greene King ***Abbot***, ***IPA***

Great Western

Sun Street, WV10 0DJ. Telephone 01902 3519090
Gaffer: Kevin Gould
Food: Home cooked Black Country food, quick and simple 12 to 2.15
Separate smoking areas
Open: 11 to 11 Mon to Sat, 12 to 3.30, 7 to 10.30 Sun

The Great Western is something of a national real ale legend. Due to its location the pub continues to attract CAMRA tickers from the whole country and beyond. It is not a footie pub, but it will be stacked out on matchdays with the archetypal real ale fans. *'Don't even try to go if this isn't your bag; leave it to those who do.'* It is easy to describe. It is '*a railway memorabilia strewn platform waiting room of a pub, but with the atmosphere and warmth of your favourite community local*.' It's difficult not to fall in love with the place and understandably the locals cherish the pub and will gladly tell you just how great it is. I will return again on another quieter lunchtime when it has never failed to deliver. The beers always include other locals to the Holden's regular ales. I wouldn't necessarily need this as their range is excellent.
UPDATE: It is intended to extend the food range on Sundays – at present it is rolls on the bar. Old Ale will be the Christmas seasonal.

BWV 21.2.05: Batham ***Best Bitter***, Downton ***Chimera***, ***Firedraft***, Holden's ***Black Country Mild***, ***Special Bitter***, ***Golden Glow***
BWV 11.11.05: Batham ***Best Bitter***, Holden's ***Black Country Bitter***, Black Country ***Mild***, ***Special Bitter***, ***Golden Glow***, ***Horndance***, Milk Street ***Autumn Gold***

Newhampton

17 Riches Street, WV6 0DW. Telephone 01902 745733
Gaffer: Bill Kendrick
Food: Seriously good home made food 12 to 9 Mon to Sat, 12 to 4 Sun
Separate smoking areas
Open: 11 to11 Mon to Thu, 11 to 12 Fri and Sat, 12 to 11 Sun

B

SP TV JB PG D

This is a grand pub in every sense of the word. Massive style, real coal fires, a bowling green garden and toilets like those found in your old primary school playground, I loved this as a place to drink. I also enjoyed looking through the many quality photos of the locals on the walls; it really makes you feel that all are welcome. Add in folk nights, a pool room and great beers and you have a pub to tell others about. On Saturdays it will be the place to get away from the crowds in town, not that it won't be busy though. As the Express and Star says it is '*a great place to come into from the cold to a roaring open fire*'. The Newhampton is easily my favourite Wolverhampton pub because it offers something for everyone, whether you are into real ale or not. The locals probably don't know just how good it is.
UPDATE: Food has expanded after last February's refurbishment. It has awards for their ciders and perry.

BWV 21.2.05: Thatcher's ***Heritage Cider***, Caledonian ***Deuchars IPA***, Kelham Island ***Pale Rider***, Courage ***Directors***, Fuller's ***London Pride***, Theakston's ***Old Peculier,*** Greene King ***Abbot***
BWV 11.11.05: Caledonian ***Deuchars IPA***, Courage ***Best***, ***Directors***, Fuller's ***London Pride***, Greene King ***Abbot***, Spinning Dog ***Mutley's Revenge***, Theakston's ***Old Peculier***, Thatcher's ***Traditional Dry Cider***

Tap and Spile

New

35 Princess Street, WV1 1HD. Telephone 01902 713319
Gaffer: Mick Stokes
Smoking Throughout
Open: 10 to 11 Mon to Sat, 10 to 10.30 Sun

MP SKY BM PG D

The Tap and Spile meets the needs of those who cannot do without a town centre pub as part of the match day experience. Other pubs nearby will probably be closed or have heavy bouncers (sorry, door personnel) but the Tap is such that the place is a home for the more gentle and rational Wolves fans who appreciate good ale.

The pub consists of a single bar that is subdivided into three separate areas. Each has varying sizes of TV all showing Sky sports (racing, on my visit). I spent the time with Elaine and Boris who were quick to let me know how they use it as the best option when shopping in town. The staff are a main feature, '*always helpful, if raving lunatics.*' They will also appeal to the students who make up a proportion of the regular pub goers. The pub has a sort of designer-distressed look, a place that many would refurbish whilst being careful not to alienate the locals who give the pub its relaxed, almost laid back atmosphere. It looks and sounds like a true town drinking den in the best traditions of that phrase.

I left to walk in the pouring rain wondering what it would be like later that evening. The same locals may possibly still be there, joined by those having the fist pint of a town centre crawl. For me I wouldn't venture far, as big bar Britain lies literally around the corner.

BWV 11.11.05: Archers ***Golden***, Banks's ***Bitter***, ***Original***, Boddingtons ***Bitter***, Salopian ***Golden Thread***, Shropshire ***Gold***, Wood ***Shropshire Lad***

Join CAMRA today and receive a free ticket to the 2007 Great British Beer Festival, Earls Court

CAMRA's recent highlights

- CAMRA was instrumental in lobbying for new flexible licensing reforms in England and Wales which allows pubs to apply for extended licenses that appeal to the local community.
- Our annual Parliamentary reception in Westminster gave us the opportunity to lobby over 100 MPs, Lords and researchers.
- CAMRA awarded their Pub Design Awards in January 2006 which gives recognition for innovative and imaginative design. CAMRA is now judging pubs that will be awarded in January 2007
- CAMRA announced their National Pub of the Year in February 2006. The award went to The Swan, Little Totham, Essex. This is the second time they have won this award!
- National Pubs Week, which encourages pubs to organise and promote events throughout the week to help reduce pub closures, was the most successful generic pub campaigns so far. Over 10,000 pubs participated in February 2005
- CAMRA has set up a Complimentary Clubs initiative which allows CAMRA members to sign up for free and receive a variety of exclusive benefits including free pint vouchers, brewery tours, competitions etc. There are currently four of these clubs – Woodforde's, Fuller's, Hook Norton and Everards. Please visit www.camra.org.uk/joinus to read more.
- Manchester hosted a successful sell-out National Winter Ales Festival
- CAMRA presented the first Cider and Perry Pub of the Year award to The Miners Arms, Lydney, Gloucester
- CAMRA has launched a number of books including the Good Beer Guide 2006, London Pub Walks, Good Pub Food, Cider Guide, Big Book of Beer and the Good Beer Guide Germany.
- CAMRA has organised over 150 beer festival around Britain

Join CAMRA today, quote '*Football Real Ale Guide*', and receive a free ticket to the 2007 Great British Beer Festival

CAMRA is offering everybody that joins CAMRA through this Football and Real Ale Guide a free 2007 Great British Beer Festival ticket. All you need to do is visit *www.camra.org.uk/joinus* or call 01727 867201 and quote '*Football Real Ale Guide*' as your promotional code.